CW01151824

Legless

*desserts to get you
in the spirit*

Kylie Banning

NEW HOLLAND

First published in Australia in 2005
This edition published in 2009 by
New Holland Publishers (Australia) Pty Ltd
London • Sydney • Auckland

www.newhollandpublishers.com
The Chandlery Unit 704 50 Westminster Bridge Road London SE1 7QY United Kingdom
1/66 Gibbes Street, Chatswood NSW 2067 Australia
5/39 Woodside Ave Northcote Auckland 0627 New Zealand

Copyright © 2005 in text: Kylie Banning
Copyright © 2005 in photographs: Andrew Ryan
Copyright © 2009 New Holland Publishers (Australia) Pty Ltd

All rights reserved. No part of this publication may be reproduced, stored in a retrieval system or transmitted, in any form or by any means, electronic, mechanical, photocopying, recording or otherwise, without the prior written permission of the publishers and copyright holders.

National Library of Australia Cataloguing-in-Publication entry:

> Banning, Kylie, 1970-
> Legless : desserts to get you in the spirit / Kylie Banning.
> Rev. ed.
> 9781741108545
>
> Desserts.
> 641.86

Publisher: Fiona Schultz
Publishing Manager: Lliane Clarke
Copy Editor: Jenny Scepanovic
Designer: Tania Gomes
Cover Designer: Domenika Fairy
Photographer: Andrew Ryan
Production Manager: Olga Dementiev
Printer: Toppan Leefung Printing Ltd (China)

10 9 8 7 6 5

Contents

Introduction	5
Cheesecakes	6
Ice-creams, sorbets and freezes	26
Cakes, tarts, puddings and trifles	62
Crepes, fondues and dipping sauces	86
Marinated fruits	98
Dessert shots	114
Jelly shots	126
Coffee treats	140
Glossary of alcoholic beverages	156
Index	158

Acknowledgements

This is a really big 'thank you' to everyone who has helped me along the way.

To my family for all their love, support and guidance with this project and anything I set out to achieve.

To Jane Jeffcott and Anna Williams—the kind of girlfriends you need in your life, who will always be your friends and help and support you through anything.

To Andrew Ryan and Lavinia Savell for such brilliant work on the photography and food styling for this book—your creativity and sense for what I was trying to achieve was amazing.

To Izzi Ali—the great listener, who will always see many solutions to any situation and who always supports and guides me. Your restaurant will be a great success.

To Michelle Cutler—for all your guidance with this book.

And to Fiona Schultz and the team at New Holland Publishers—thank you so much for making this dream a reality and for helping to put this book in everybody's kitchen!

Introduction

At how many parties have you been offered a boring piece of chocolate cake or fruit flan for dessert? On these occasions, how many guests even bother to eat their serve? Decadent Desserts provides the quick and delicious solution. Guaranteed to liven up any type of party, these desserts contain the extra special ingredient that will inject excitement and festivity into your party—that's right, it's alcohol. These recipes all use your favourite alcoholic liqueurs and spirits to ensure your party ends with a bang.

Whatever the occasion and whatever the season, this book contains the dessert that will add the perfect touch to your party. Simply because your party is a formal sit-down dinner doesn't mean it has to be dull and stuffy. Impress your audience and give the party a sparkle by serving dessert with a twist. Gone are the days of apple crumble—the Pear and Chambord Crumble will make your party one to remember.

If the party is a lively cocktail event, guests will be lining up for some Chi Chi or Midori Splice Jelly Shots, not only because they're new and exciting but also because they taste divine. On a summer's afternoon after a barbecue lunch, cool down with refreshing Strawberry and Lychee Cream Freeze or a Liquid Ecstasy Pineapple Boat.

There are simply so many wonderful desserts to choose from in this inspirational collection that your biggest problem will be deciding which one to make first.

Taste and excitement are not the only advantages to using these recipes. They are all designed to be quick and easy to make—you certainly don't need to be a qualified chef to make them to perfection.

The range of desserts also provides you with a number of different preparation options. Whether you prefer baking or simply refrigerating to set, there is something in here for everyone. Just as importantly, the desserts can all be prepared in advance to alleviate your worry when the party begins.

Enjoy making and eating these delectable and fun desserts. They are sure to be the icing on the cake at your next party.

Please note: some photos have been taken during preparation and may not always reflect the final presentation of the dessert.

Cheesecakes

A collection of indulgent, luscious cheesecakes with no baking involved.
And to spice things up, add a dash of alcohol for the perfect end to a meal ...

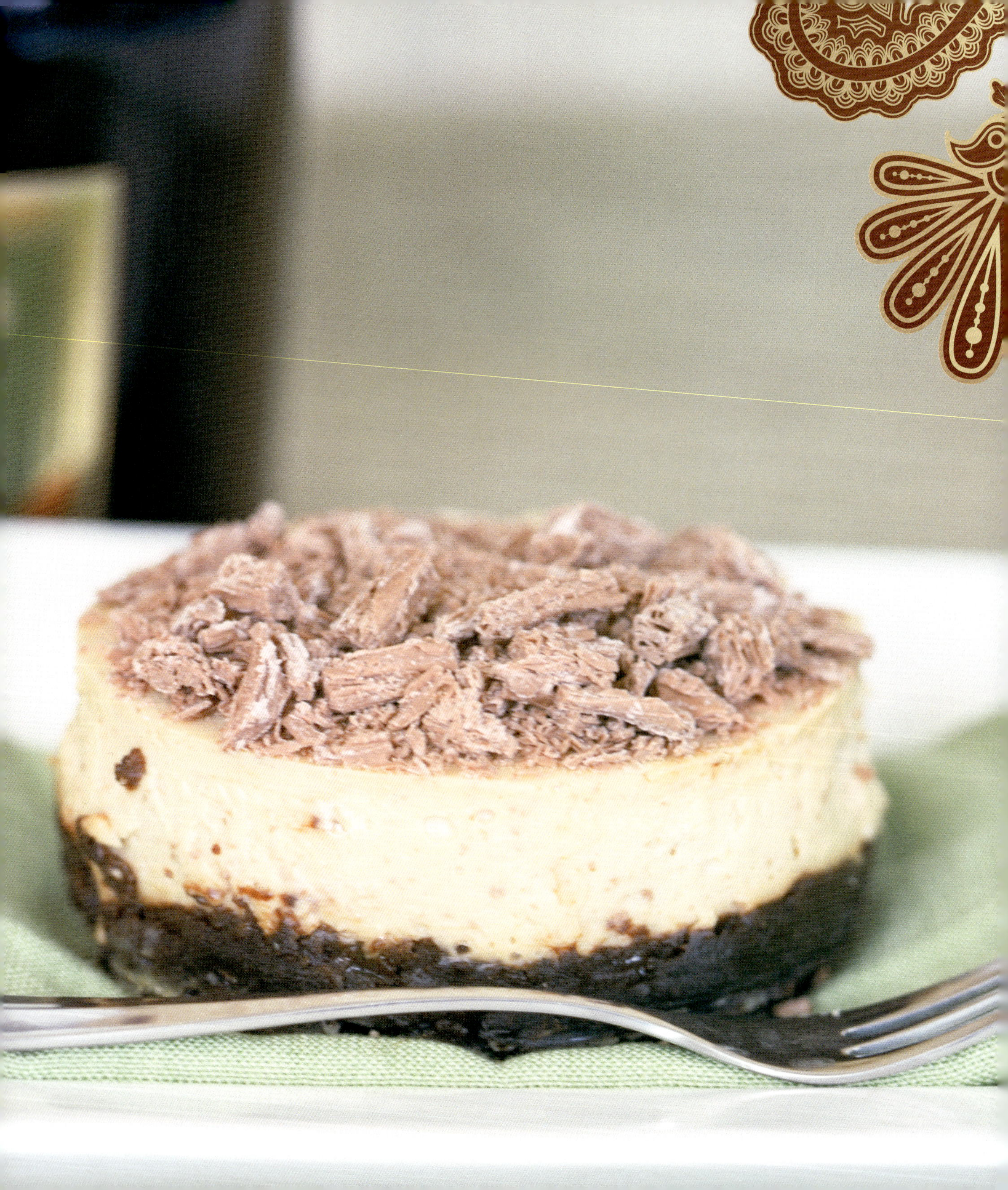

Baileys Irish Cream Cheesecake

Serves 10

Base
250 g (8 oz) chocolate biscuits
125 g (4 oz) butter

Filling
125 ml (½ cup) boiling water
1 tablespoon gelatin
180 g (6 oz) sugar
1 tablespoon lemon juice
250 g (8 oz) cream cheese
300 ml (1½ cups) cream
180 ml (¾ cup) Baileys Irish Cream
1 x 30 g (1 oz) flakey chocolate bar

To make base: Crush biscuits into very fine pieces. Melt butter and add to crushed biscuits, mix well and press into a springform cheesecake tin, packing mixture tightly to form a crust. Refrigerate to set.

To make filling: Sprinkle the gelatin over the boiling water, stir until dissolved and leave to cool. Place sugar and lemon juice in a blender and mix lightly. Add room temperature cream cheese and continue to blend. Add cooled gelatin mix, cream and Baileys and blend until smooth and mixed well.

Crumble half the chocolate bar into mixture and stir through lightly. Pour over base. Crumble remaining chocolate bar over top of cheesecake. Refrigerate to set.

Black Forest Cheesecake

Serves 10

Base
250 g (8 oz) chocolate biscuits
125 g (4 oz) butter

Filling
125 ml (½ cup) boiling water
1 tablespoon gelatin
180 g (6 oz) sugar
1 tablespoon lemon juice
250 g (8 oz) cream cheese
300 ml (1½ cups) cream
125 ml (½ cup) Crème de Cacao
1 x 425 g (12½ oz) can pitted black cherries (reserve syrup for topping)

Topping
1 tablespoon cornflour
1 tablespoon sugar
Syrup from the can of black cherries
60 ml (¼ cup) Crème de Cassis

To make base: Crush biscuits into very fine pieces. Melt butter and add to crushed biscuits, mix well and press into a springform cheesecake tin, packing mixture tightly to form a crust. Refrigerate to set.

To make filling: Sprinkle the gelatin over the boiling water, stir until dissolved and leave to cool. Place sugar and lemon juice in a blender and mix lightly. Add room temperature cream cheese and continue to blend. Add cooled gelatin mix, cream and Crème de Cacao and blend until smooth and mixed well.

Pour one-third of the mixture over the base. Drain the can of cherries, reserving syrup. Spread half of the can of cherries over mixture. Spread one-third of the mixture over cherries, then place remainder of cherries over the mixture. Use the last of the mixture over the top of the cherries. Refrigerate to set.

To make topping: Place cornflour and sugar into saucepan, gradually stir in reserved syrup, stir until boiling then remove from heat. Add Crème de Cassis, continue stirring for a few minutes to allow mixture to cool slightly. Spread topping over cheesecake. Swirl lightly into mixture. Refrigerate to set.

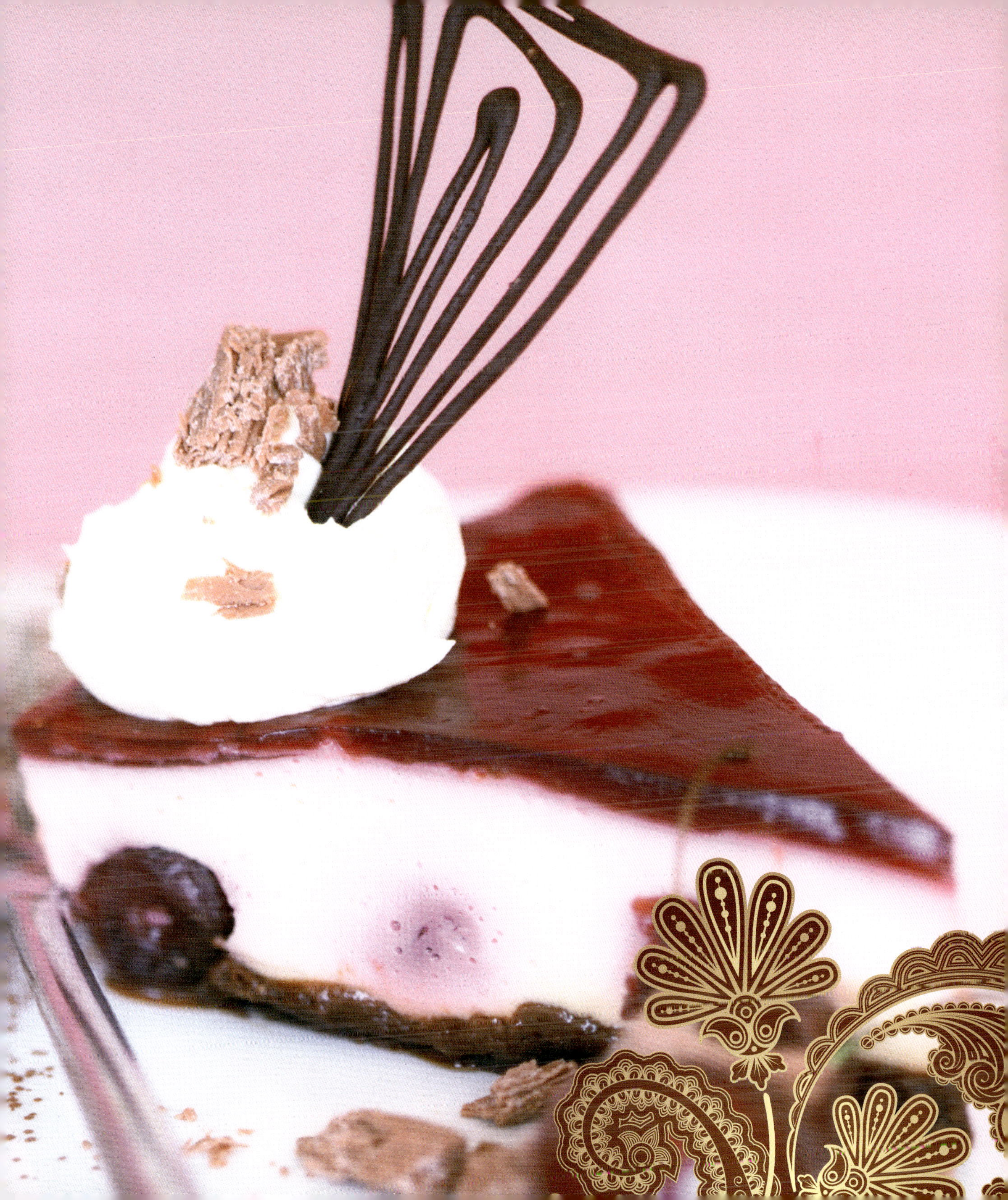

Frangelico Cheesecake

Serves 10

Base
250 g (8 oz) chocolate biscuits
125 g (4 oz) butter

Filling
125 ml (½ cup) boiling water
1 tablespoon gelatin
180 g (6 oz) sugar
1 tablespoon lemon juice
250 g (8 oz) cream cheese
300 ml (1½ cups) cream
180 ml (¾ cup) Frangelico
1 x 30 g (1 oz) flakey chocolate bar

To make base: Crush biscuits into very fine pieces. Melt butter and add to crushed biscuits, mix well and press into a springform cheesecake tin, packing mixture tightly to form a crust. Refrigerate to set.

To make filling: Sprinkle the gelatin over the boiling water, stir until dissolved and leave to cool.

Place sugar and lemon juice in a blender and mix lightly. Add room temperature cream cheese and continue to blend. Add cooled gelatin mix, cream and Frangelico and blend until smooth and mixed well.

Crumble half the chocolate bar into mixture and stir through lightly, pour over base. Crumble remaining chocolate bar evenly over top of cheesecake. Refrigerate to set.

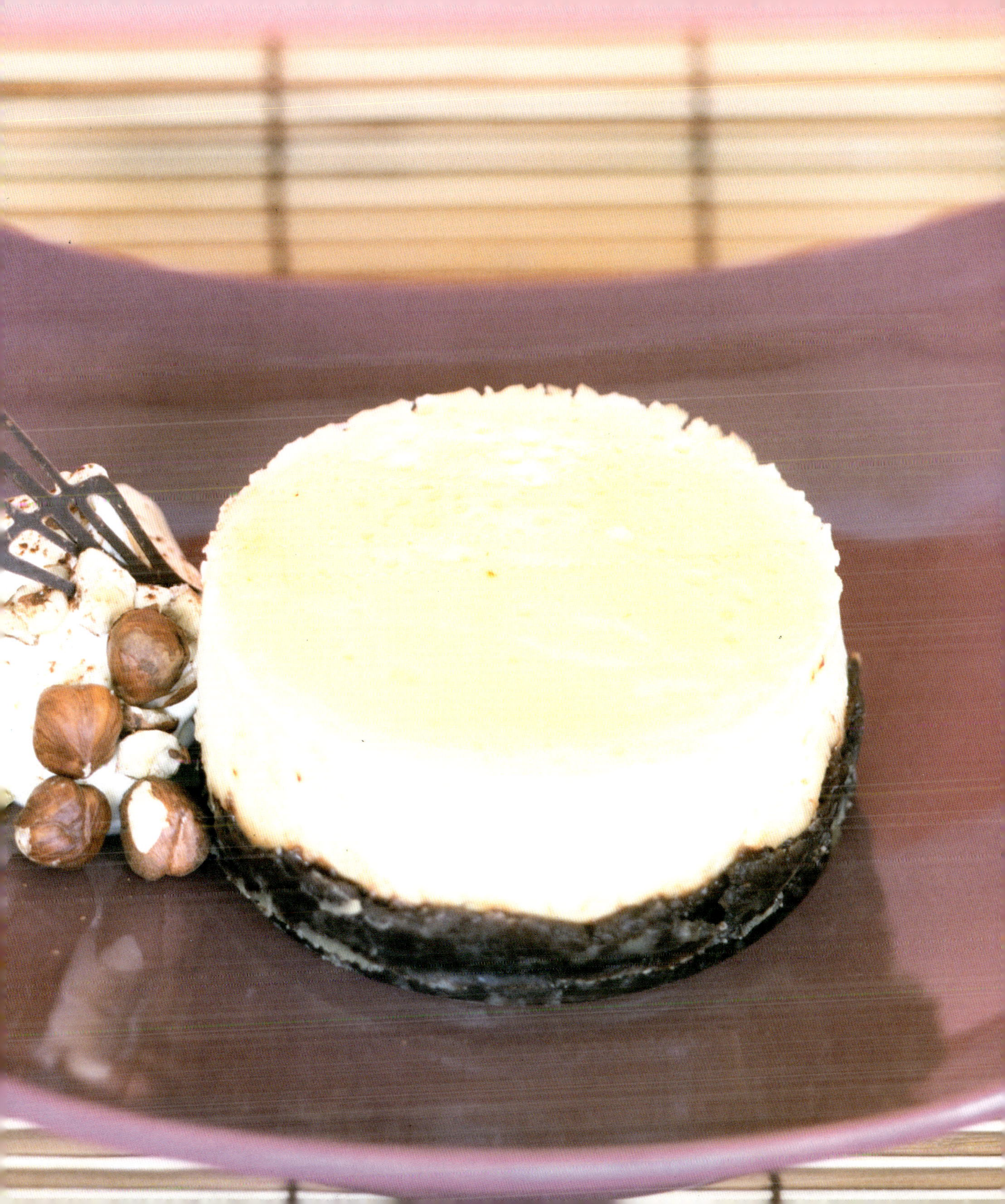

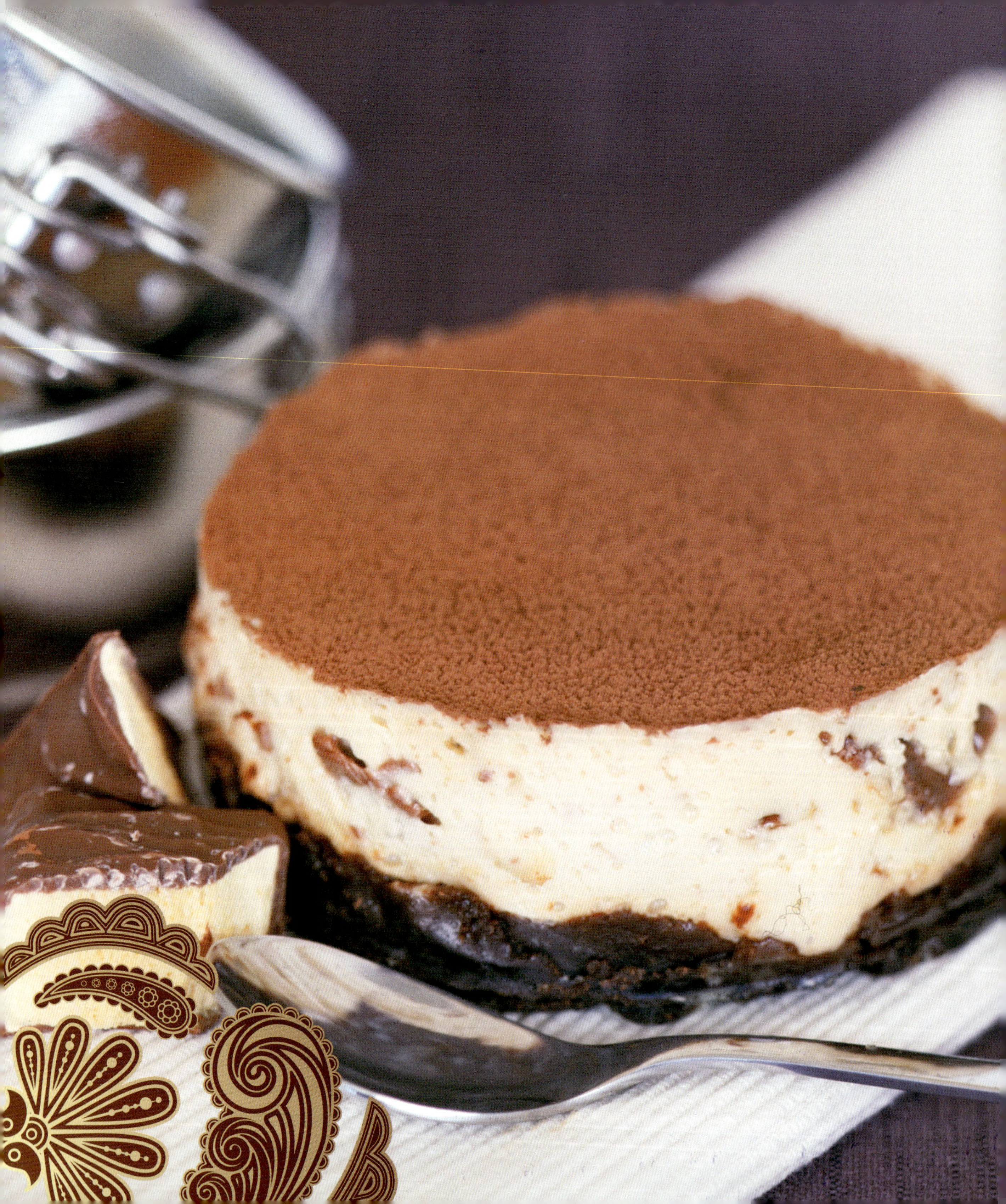

Honeycomb Cheesecake

Serves 10

Base
250 g (8 oz) chocolate biscuits
125 g (4 oz) butter

Filling
125 ml (½ cup) boiling water
1 tablespoon gelatin
180 g (6 oz) sugar
1 tablespoon lemon juice
250 g (8 oz) cream cheese
300 ml (1½ cups) cream
1 x 50 g (2 oz) chocolate honeycomb bar
90 ml (30 fl oz) Baileys Irish Cream
90 ml (30 fl oz) butterscotch liqueur or butterscotch schnapps

To make base: Crush biscuits into very fine pieces. Melt butter and add to crushed biscuits, mix well and press into a springform cheesecake tin, packing mixture tightly to form a crust. Refrigerate to set.

To make filling: Sprinkle the gelatin over the boiling water, stir until dissolved and leave to cool.

Place sugar and lemon juice in a blender and mix lightly. Add room temperature cream cheese and continue to blend. Add cooled gelatin mix, cream and liqueur and blend until smooth and mixed well.

Crumble the chocolate honeycomb bar into mixture and stir through lightly, pour over base. Refrigerate to set.

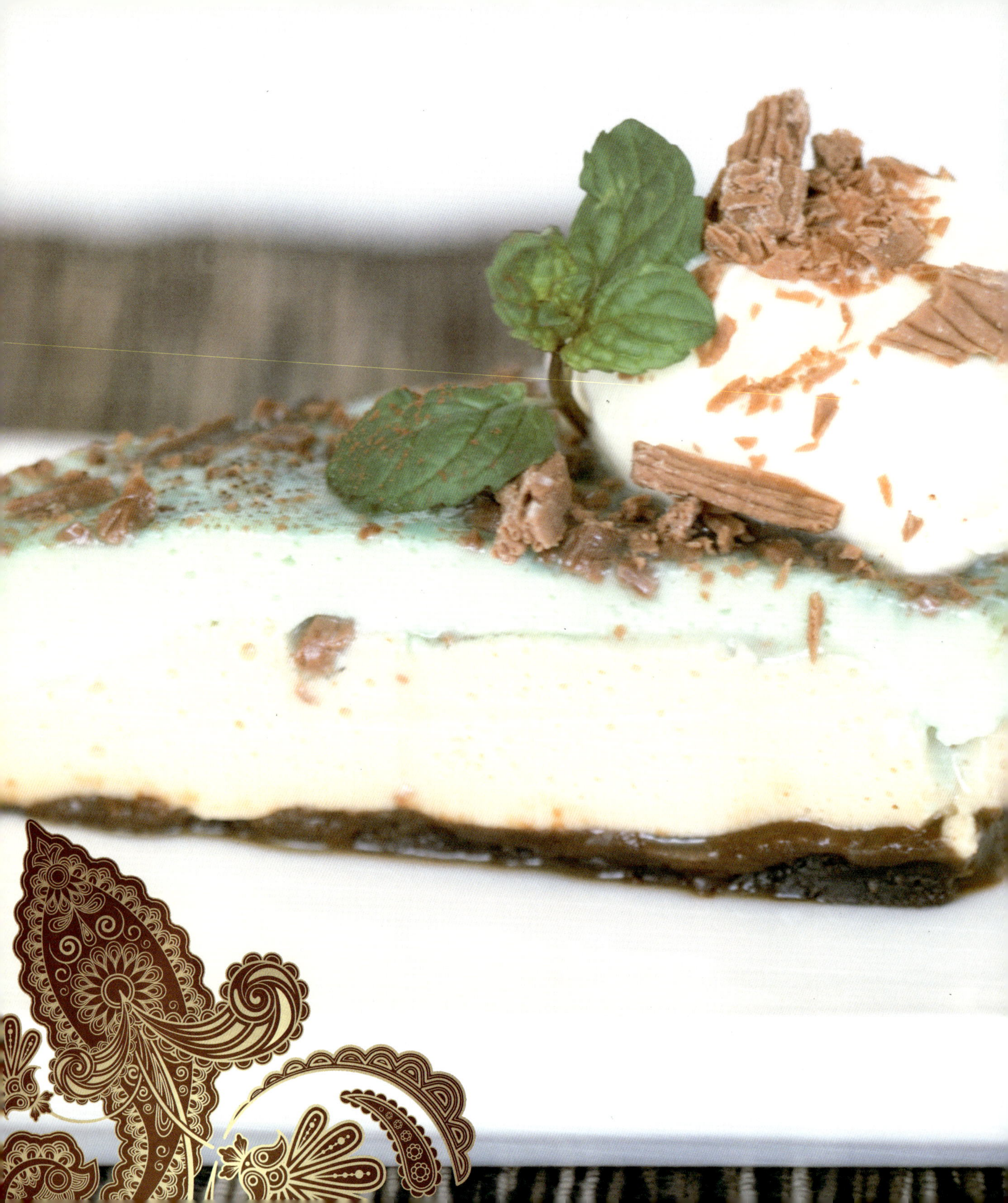

Choc Mint Cheesecake

Serves 10

Base
250 g (8 oz) chocolate biscuits
125 g (4 oz) butter

Filling
125 ml (½ cup) boiling water
1 tablespoon gelatin
180 g (6 oz) sugar
1 tablespoon lemon juice
250 g (8 oz) cream cheese
300 ml (1½ cups) cream
1 x 35 g (1 oz) mint crisp chocolate bar
30 ml (1 fl oz) Baileys Irish Cream
60 ml (¼ cup) Brown Crème de Cacao
45 ml (1½ fl oz) Crème de Menthe

To make base: Crush biscuits into very fine pieces. Melt butter and add to crushed biscuits, mix well and press into a springform cheesecake tin, packing mixture tightly to form a crust. Refrigerate to set.

To make filling: Sprinkle the gelatin over the boiling water, stir until dissolved and leave to cool.

Place sugar and lemon juice in a blender and mix lightly. Add room temperature cream cheese and continue to blend. Add cooled gelatin mix and cream and blend until smooth and mixed well.

Divide mixture in two. Add Crème de Cacao and Baileys to the first half and blend, then pour the mixture over the base. Crumble half the mint chip chocolate bar onto the first half of the mixture. Place in the refrigerator to set slightly.

Return the second half of the mixture to the blender and add the Crème de Menthe and blend well. Pour very gently onto the top of the first half so that you layer the cheesecake. Crumble the remaining chocolate bar over the mixture. Refrigerate to set.

Strawberries, Cointreau and Cream Cheesecake

Serves 10

Base
250 g (8 oz) plain biscuits
125 g (4 oz) butter

Strawberries
1 punnet strawberries
60 ml (¼ cup) Cointreau
1 teaspoon castor sugar

Filling
125 ml (½ cup) boiling water
1 tablespoon gelatin
180 g (6 oz) sugar
1 tablespoon lemon juice
250 g (8 oz) cream cheese
300 ml (1½ cups) cream
125 ml (½ cup) strawberry liqueur

To make base: Crush biscuits into very fine pieces. Melt butter and add to crushed biscuits, mix well and press into a springform cheesecake tin, packing mixture tightly to form a crust. Refrigerate to set.

To prepare strawberries: Trim tops from strawberries and cut in half, place into a bowl. Add 60 ml (¼ cup) Cointreau and the castor sugar to the bowl and toss to coat strawberries well.

To make filling: Sprinkle the gelatin over the boiling water, stir until dissolved and leave to cool.

Place sugar and lemon juice in a blender and mix lightly. Add room temperature cream cheese and continue to blend. Add cooled gelatin mix, strawberry liqueur, drained Cointreau and juice from the strawberries, and cream and blend until smooth and mixed well.

Pour half of the mixture onto the biscuit base then top with two-thirds of the strawberries. Cover with the remaining cheesecake mix. Refrigerate to set.

Keep the remaining strawberries in the refrigerator to use as a garnish when you serve the cheesecake.

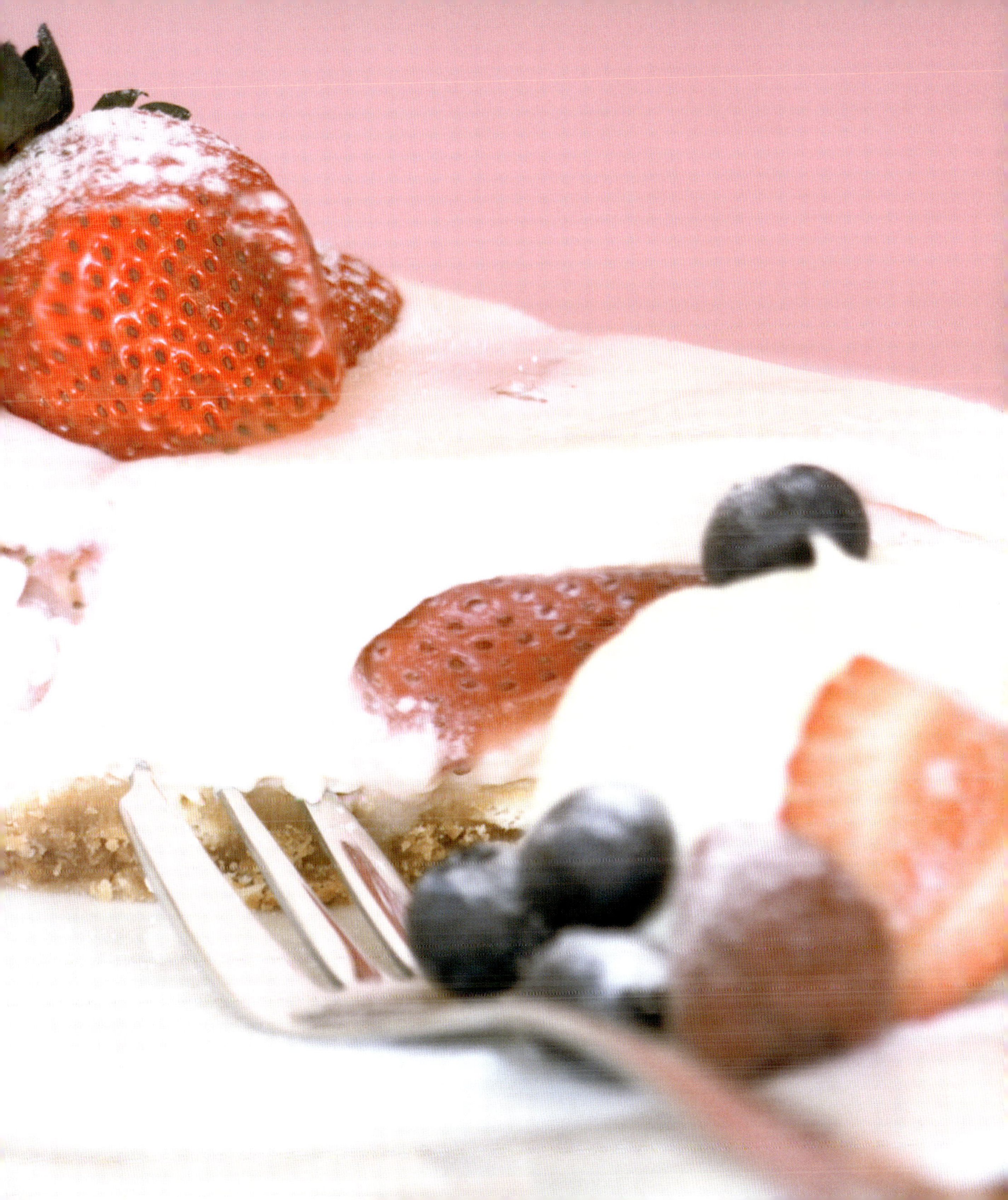

Mixed Berry Cheesecake

Serves 10

Base
250 g (8 oz) plain biscuits
125 g (4 oz) butter

Filling
125 ml (½ cup) boiling water
1 tablespoon gelatin
180 g (6 oz) sugar
1 tablespoon lemon juice
250 g (8 oz) cream cheese
300 ml (1½ cups) cream
90 ml (⅓ cup) Chambord

Topping
½ punnet strawberries
1 punnet blackberries or raspberries or both
150 ml (⅔ cup) cranberry juice
90 ml (⅓ cup) Chambord
1 tablespoon castor sugar
1 tablespoon cornflour

To make base: Crush biscuits into very fine pieces. Melt butter and add to crushed biscuits, mix well and press into a springform cheesecake tin, packing mixture tightly to form a crust. Refrigerate to set.

To make filling: Sprinkle the gelatin over the boiling water, stir until dissolved and leave to cool. Place sugar and lemon juice in a blender and mix lightly. Add room temperature cream cheese and continue to blend. Add cooled gelatin mix, cream and Chambord and blend until smooth and mixed well. Pour cheesecake mix over base. Refrigerate to set.

To make topping: Trim tops from strawberries and cut in half. Arrange around the outside of the cheesecake tin with points up and the outsides of the strawberries against the tin. Wash the blackberries and/or raspberries and fill the middle of the strawberry arrangement. Place cranberry juice, Chambord and castor sugar in a saucepan and bring to the boil. Blend the cornflour with a small amount of cold water and mix well. Add to the mixture in the saucepan stirring continuously until it has thickened, remove from heat. Allow to cool slightly, and then pour gently over the arranged fruit. This will set the fruit in place like a jelly. Refrigerate to set.

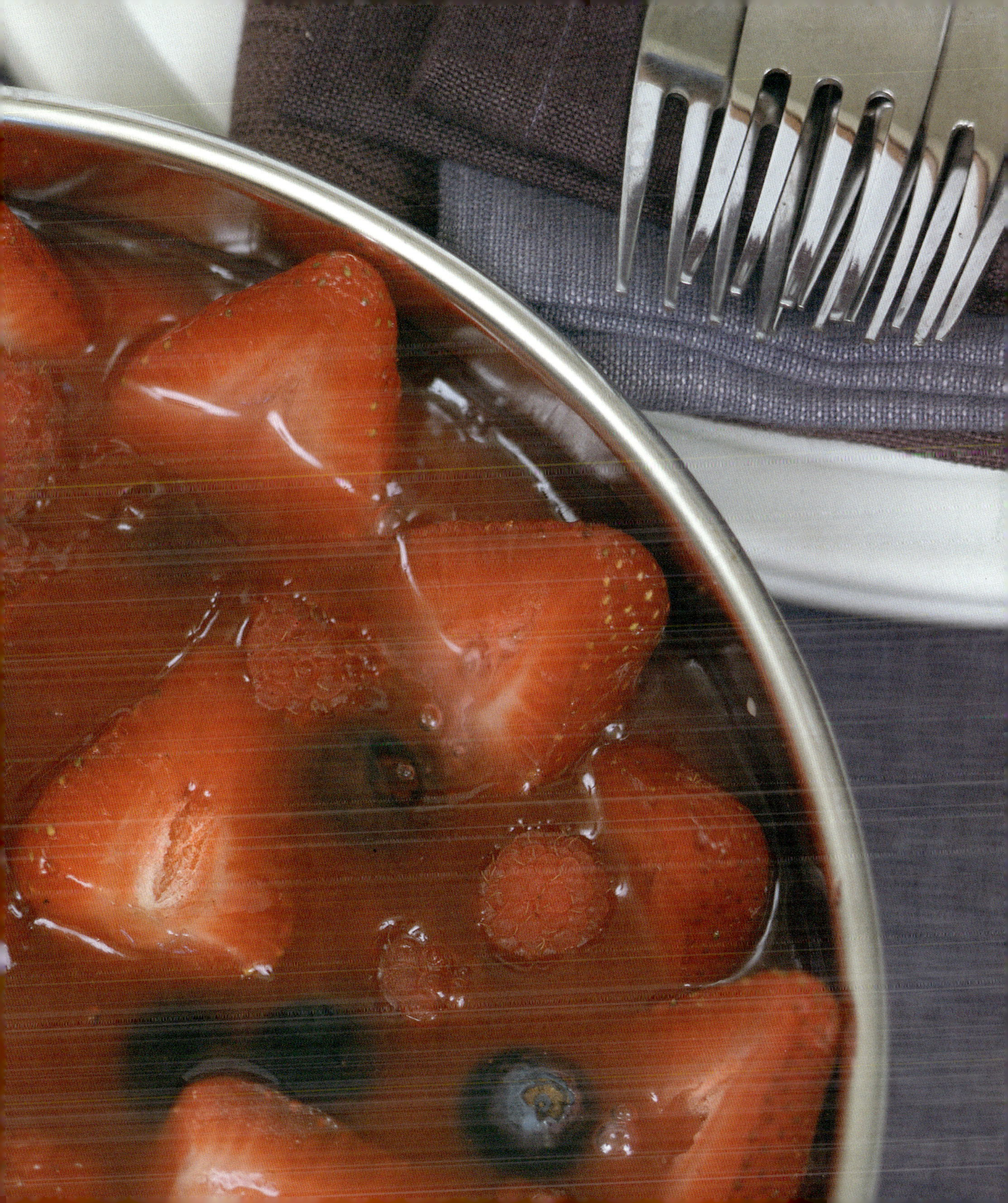

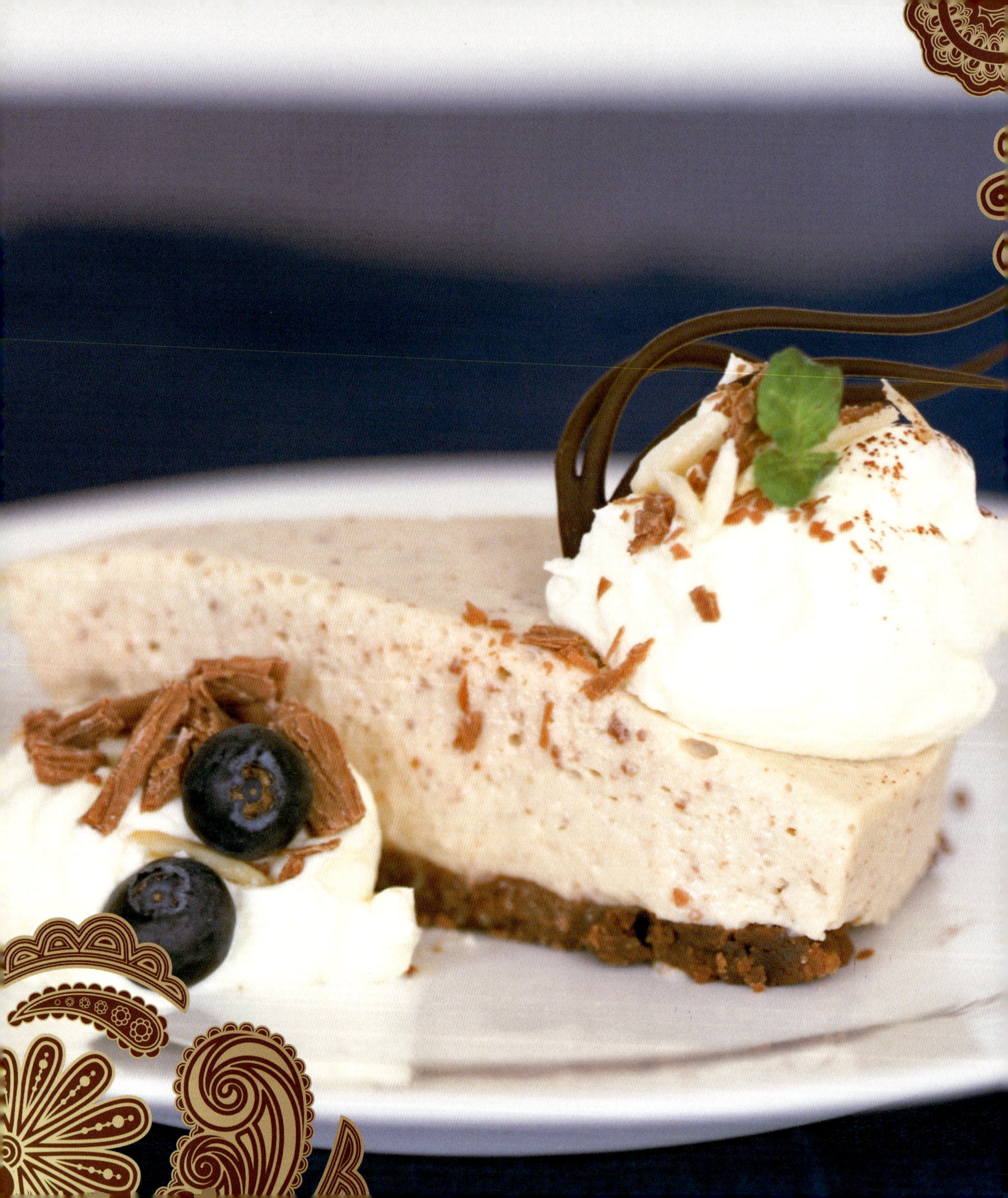

Toblerone Cheesecake

Serves 10

Base
250 g (8 oz) chocolate biscuits
125 g (4 oz) butter

Filling
125 ml (½ cup) boiling water
1 tablespoon gelatin
180 g (6 oz) sugar
1 tablespoon lemon juice
250 g (8 oz) cream cheese
300 ml (1½ cups) cream
1 tablespoon honey
60 ml (¼ cup) Frangelico
60 ml (½ cup) Baileys Irish Cream
60 ml (½ cup) Brown Crème de Cacao
1 x 50 g (2 oz) Toblerone chocolate bar

To make base: Crush biscuits into very fine pieces. Melt butter and add to crushed biscuits, mix well and press into a springform cheesecake tin, packing mixture tightly to form a crust. Refrigerate to set.

To prepare filling: Sprinkle the gelatin over the boiling water, stir until dissolved and leave to cool.

Place sugar and lemon juice in a blender and mix lightly. Add room temperature cream cheese and continue to blend. Add cooled gelatin mix and cream, honey and alcohol and blend until smooth and mixed well.

Crumble the chocolate bar into mixture and pulse blend to crush slightly, pour over base. Refrigerate to set.

Ginger, Lychee and Orange Cheesecake

Serves 10

Base
250 g (8 oz) ginger biscuits
125 g (4 oz) butter

Filling
125 ml (½ cup) boiling water
1 tablespoon gelatin
180 g (6 oz) sugar
1 tablespoon lemon juice
250 g (8 oz) cream cheese
300 ml (1½ cups) cream
425 g (12½ oz) can lychees (reserve syrup for topping)
90 ml (⅓ cup) Paraiso lychee liqueur

Topping
1 tablespoon castor sugar
1 tablespoon cornflour
Syrup from the can of lychees
90 ml (⅓ cup) Orange Curacao

To make base: Crush biscuits into very fine pieces. Melt butter and add to crushed biscuits, mix well and press into a springform cheesecake tin, packing mixture tightly to form a crust. Refrigerate to set.

To prepare filling: Sprinkle the gelatin over the boiling water, stir until dissolved and leave to cool.

Place sugar and lemon juice in a blender and mix lightly. Add room temperature cream cheese and continue to blend. Add cooled gelatin mix, cream and liqueur and blend until smooth and mixed well.

Pour one-third of the mixture over base. Drain the can of lychees, reserving syrup. Spread half of the can of lychees over the mixture. Spread one-third of the mixture over lychees, place remainder of lychees over mixture. Use the last of the mixture over lychees. Refrigerate to set.

To make topping: Place sugar and cornflour into a saucepan, gradually stir in reserved syrup, stir until boiling then remove from heat. Add Orange Curacao and continue stirring for a few minutes to allow mixture to cool slightly, then spread topping over cheesecake. Swirl lightly into mixture. Refrigerate to set.

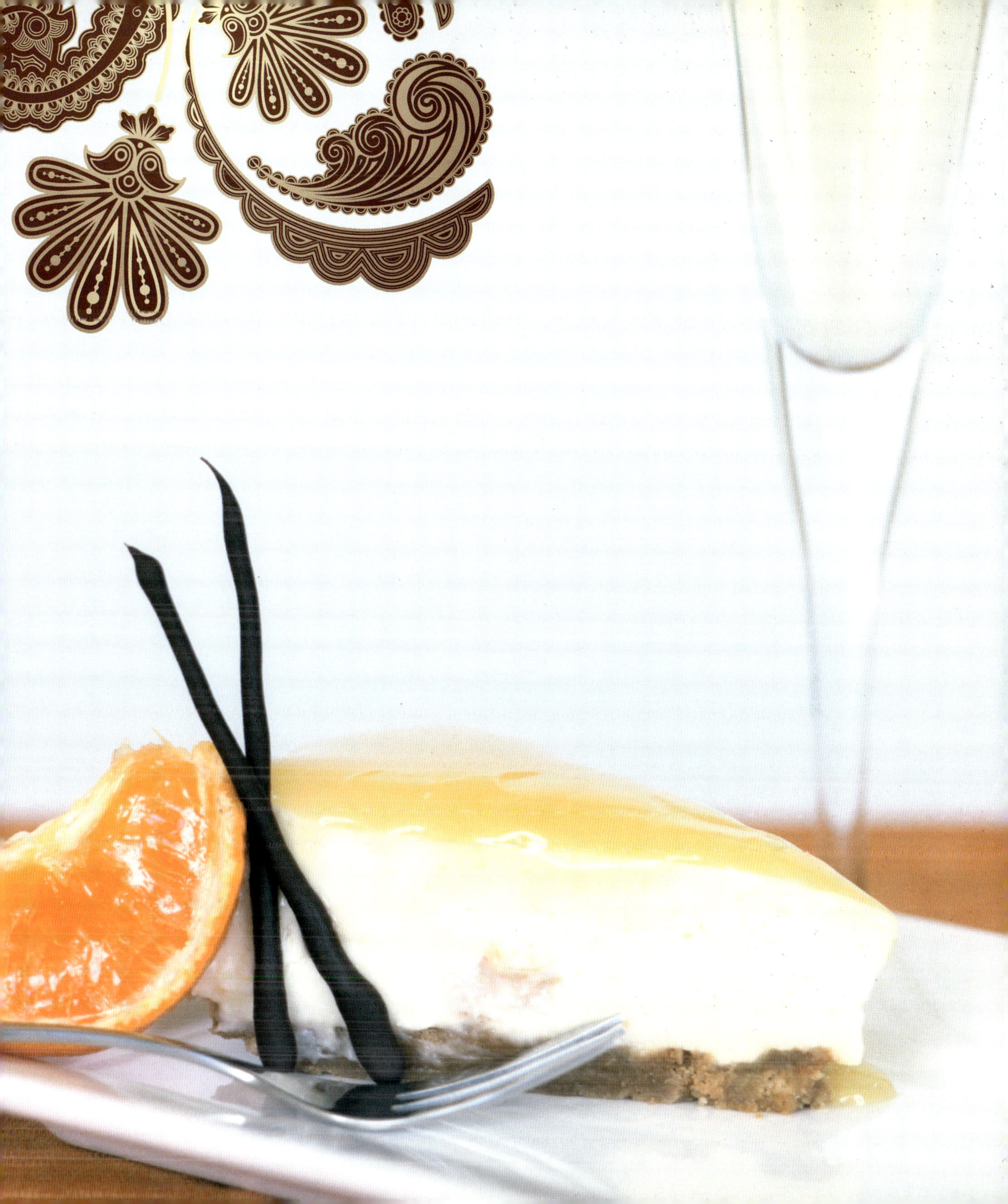

Ice-creams, sorbets and freezes

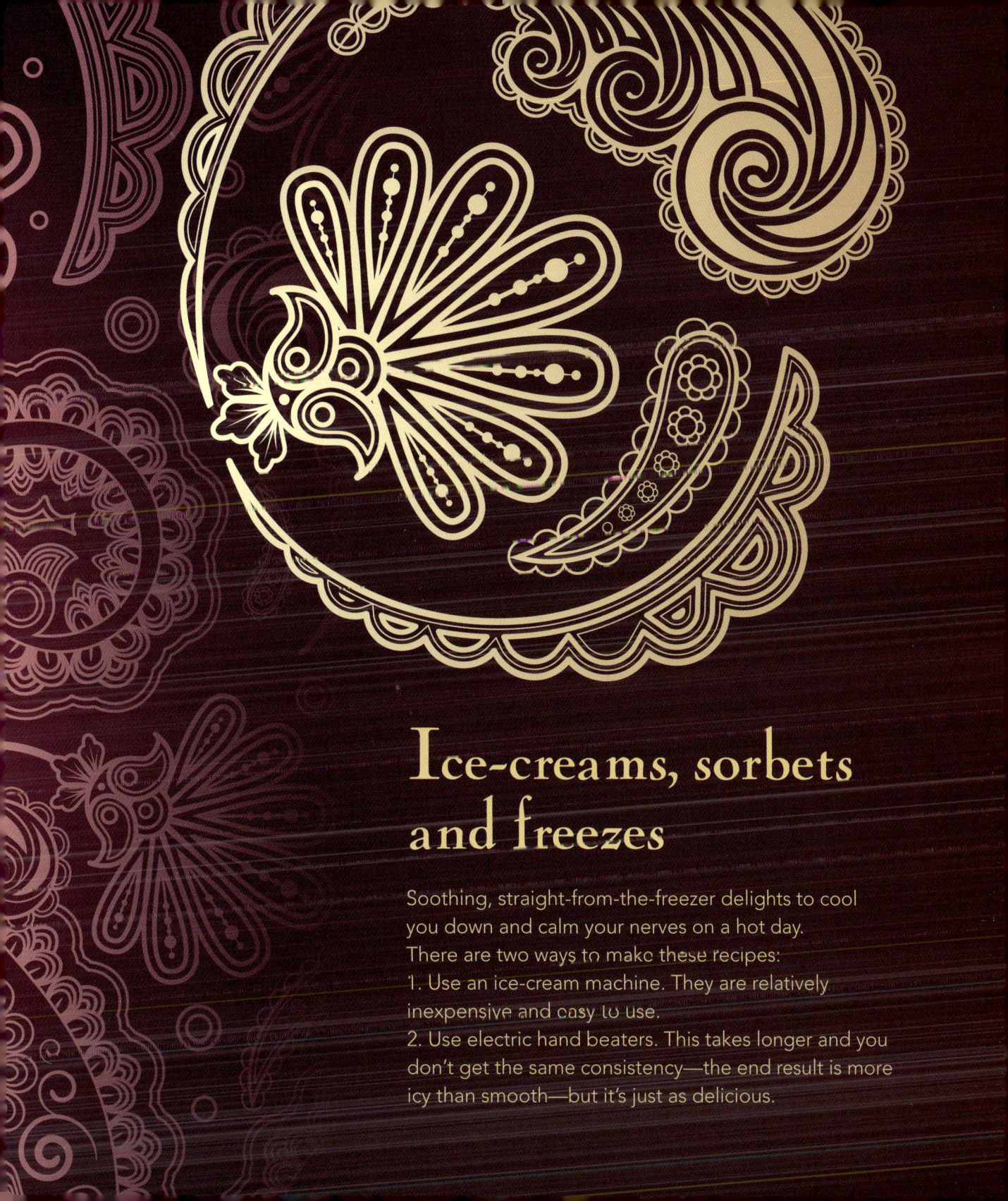

Soothing, straight-from-the-freezer delights to cool you down and calm your nerves on a hot day. There are two ways to make these recipes:
1. Use an ice-cream machine. They are relatively inexpensive and easy to use.
2. Use electric hand beaters. This takes longer and you don't get the same consistency—the end result is more icy than smooth—but it's just as delicious.

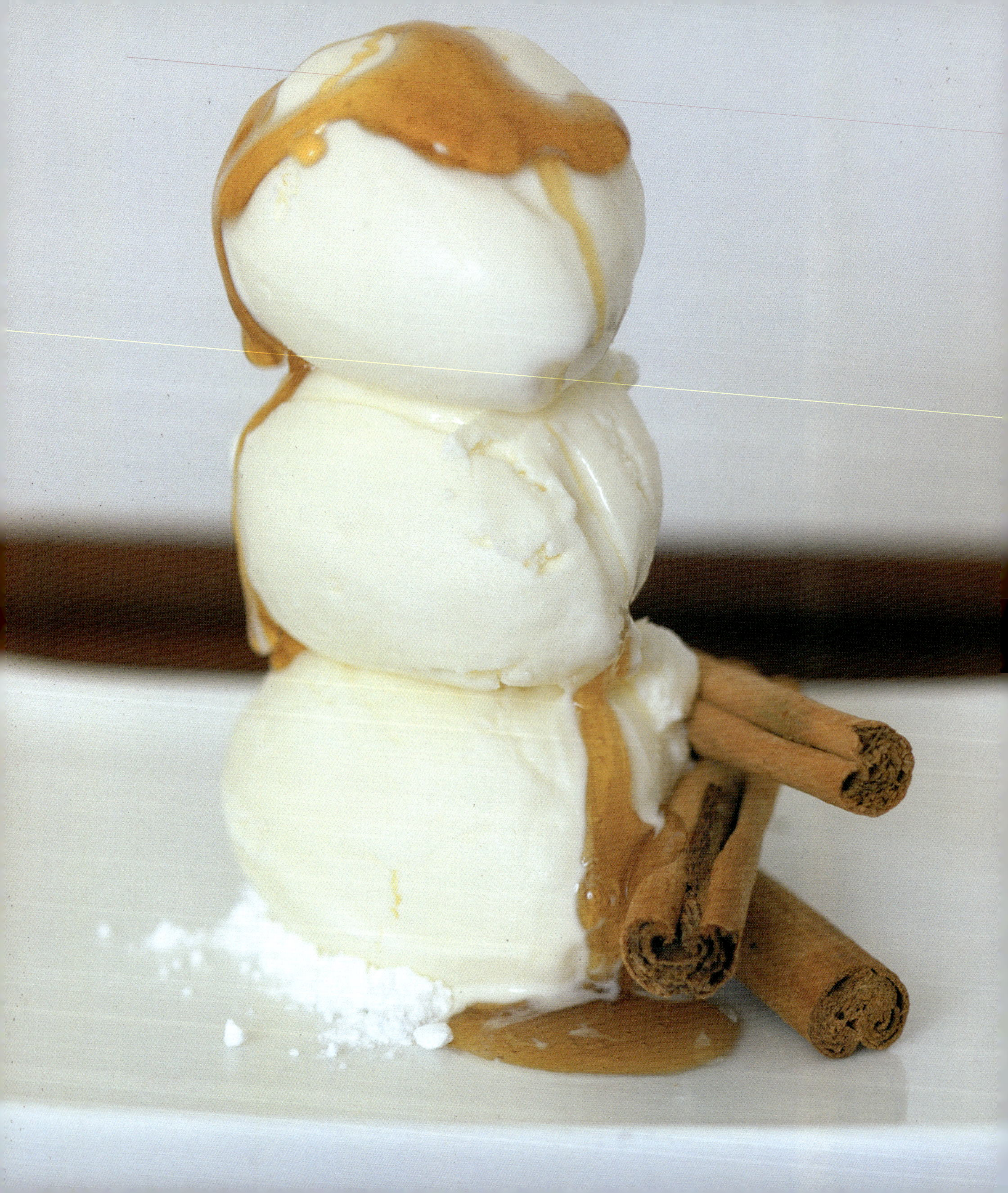

Honey, Cream and Cinnamon Ice-cream

Makes approximately 1.5 litres (4 cups)

1 vanilla bean, split
400 ml (1¾ cups) cream
310 ml (1½ cups) milk
6 egg yolks
200 ml (7 fl oz) honey
1 teaspoon ground cinnamon
300 ml (1½ cups) cream, extra
90 ml (⅓ cup) Medos Honey Vodka

Place the vanilla bean, cream and milk into a saucepan and bring to the boil. Beat the egg yolks with the honey and cinnamon until pale and creamy, then slowly whisk into the cream mixture until blended. Place the mixture into a clean bowl and stand over a pot of simmering water, stirring constantly until the mixture coats the back of a wooden spoon. Strain into a bowl and allow to cool.

Stir in the extra cream and vodka then pour into a stainless steel bowl and freeze. Stir every two hours until firm then transfer to a suitable container to freeze. Alternatively place all chilled ingredients into your ice-cream machine and leave to churn and freeze.

White Chocolate and Coconut Ice-cream

Makes approximately 750 ml (3 cups)

3 egg yolks
2 tablespoon brown sugar
200 g (6½ oz) white chocolate
300 ml (1½ cups) coconut cream
300 ml (1½ cups) thickened cream
2 tablespoons desiccated coconut
60 ml (¼ cup) Malibu

Whisk egg yolks and sugar in a bowl over hot water until thick and pale. Keeping over the heat, break up the white chocolate into small pieces and place in the egg mixture, whisk until the chocolate melts then whisk coconut cream into egg mixture.

Take off the heat and fold cream, coconut and Malibu into mixture. Pour into a loaf tin, cover in cling film and freeze for approximately five hours. Alternatively place all chilled ingredients into your ice-cream machine and leave to churn and freeze.

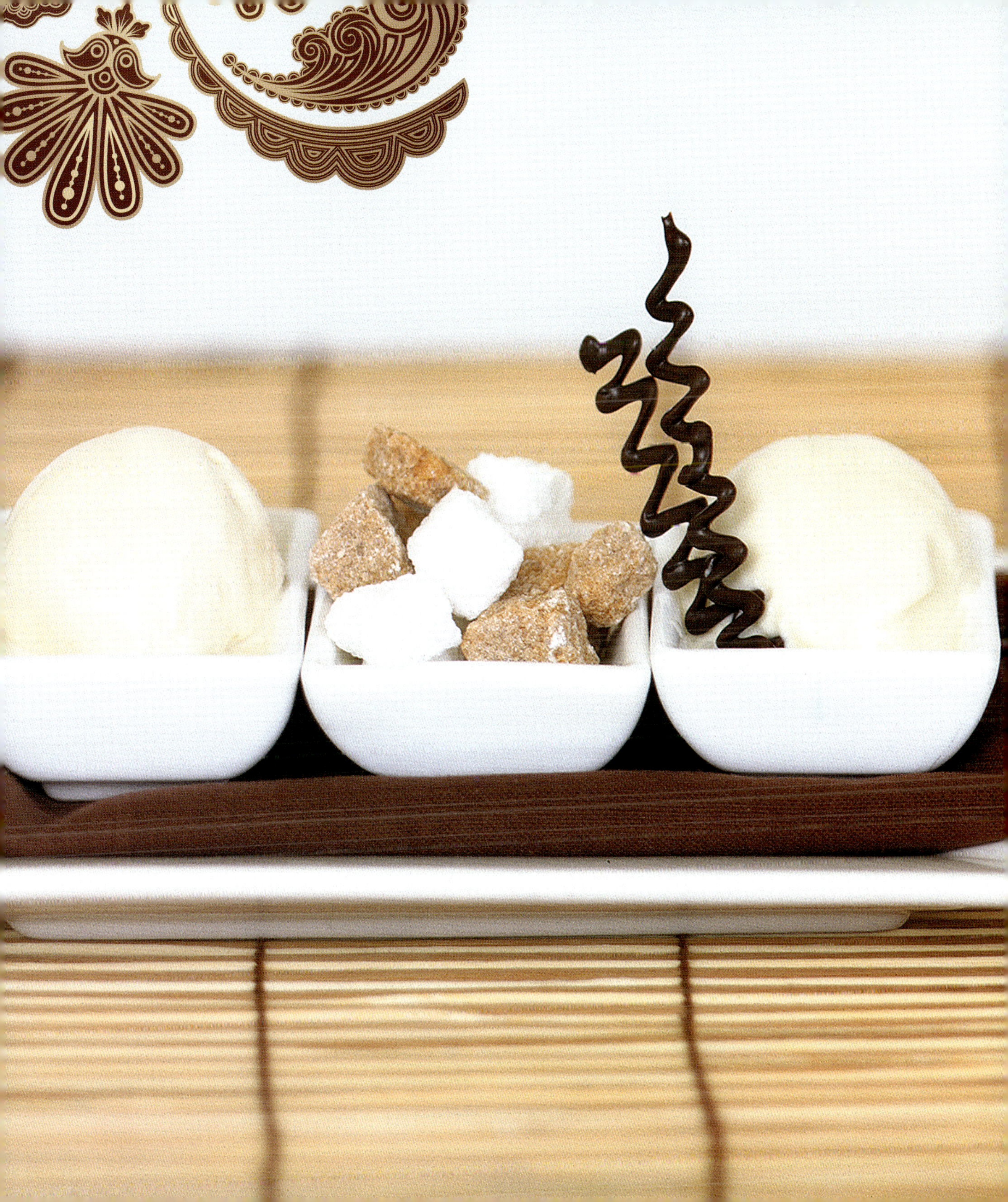

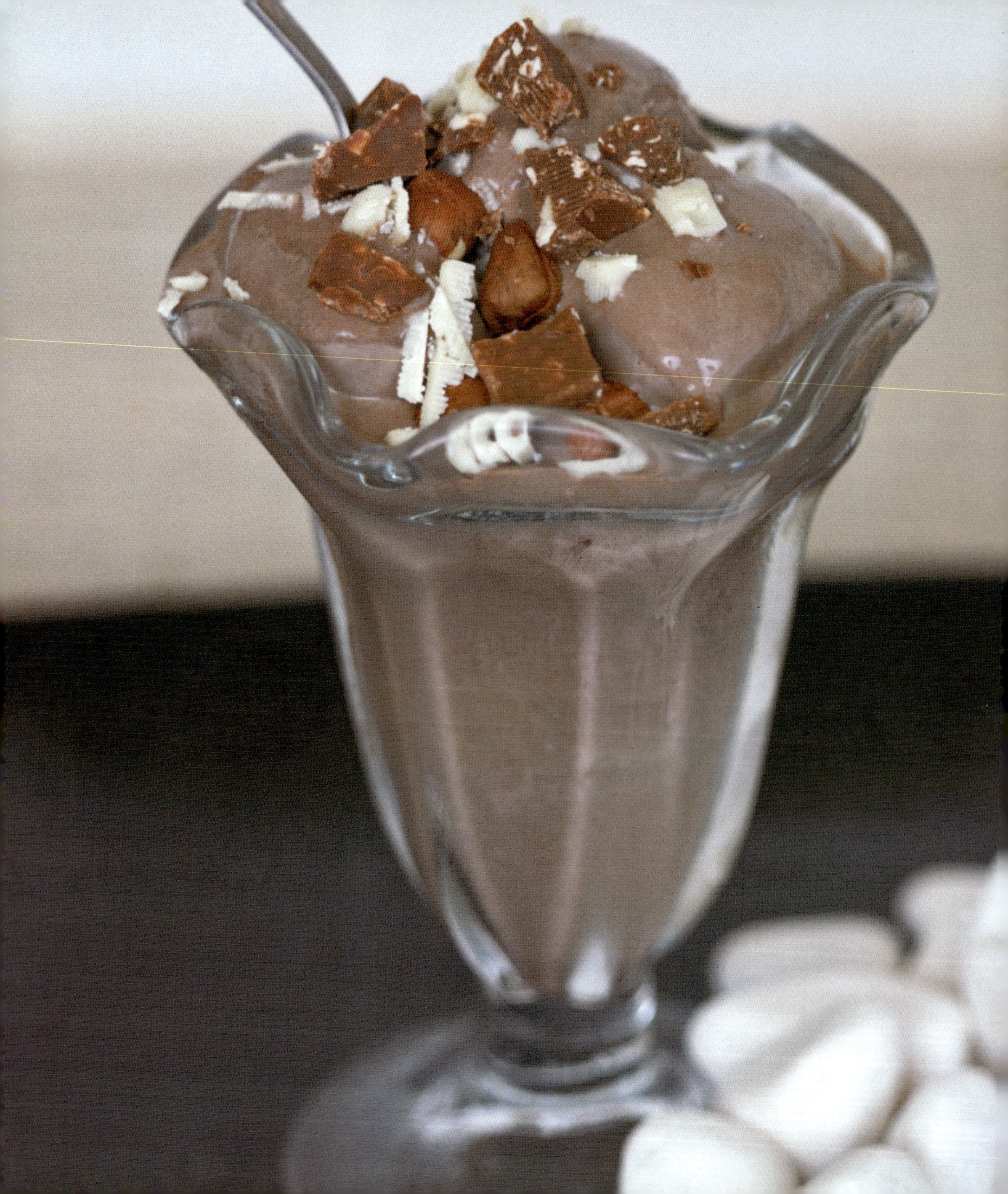

Swiss Chocolate Ice-cream

Note: This recipe works best with an ice-cream machine.

125 ml (½ cup) castor sugar
60 g (2 oz) cocoa
250 ml (1 cup) milk
2 egg yolks
1 x 50 g (2 oz) Toblerone chocolate bar
200 ml (7 fl oz) cream
60 ml (¼ cup) Crème de Cacao
30 ml (1 fl oz) Frangelico
1 tablespoon honey

Makes approximately 750 ml (3 cups)

Place sugar, cocoa and half the milk in a saucepan and heat gently. Combine remaining milk and egg yolks then add to the mixture. Bring mixture gently to the boil, stirring constantly. Remove from heat and allow to cool

Add the Toblerone chocolate bar to the hot mixture so that the chocolate partly melts, stirring occasionally. The mixture will resemble custard. Refrigerate overnight.

The following day add cream, Crème de Cacao, Frangelico and honey and mix with a wire whisk. Pour chilled mixture into the ice-cream machine and leave to churn and freeze.

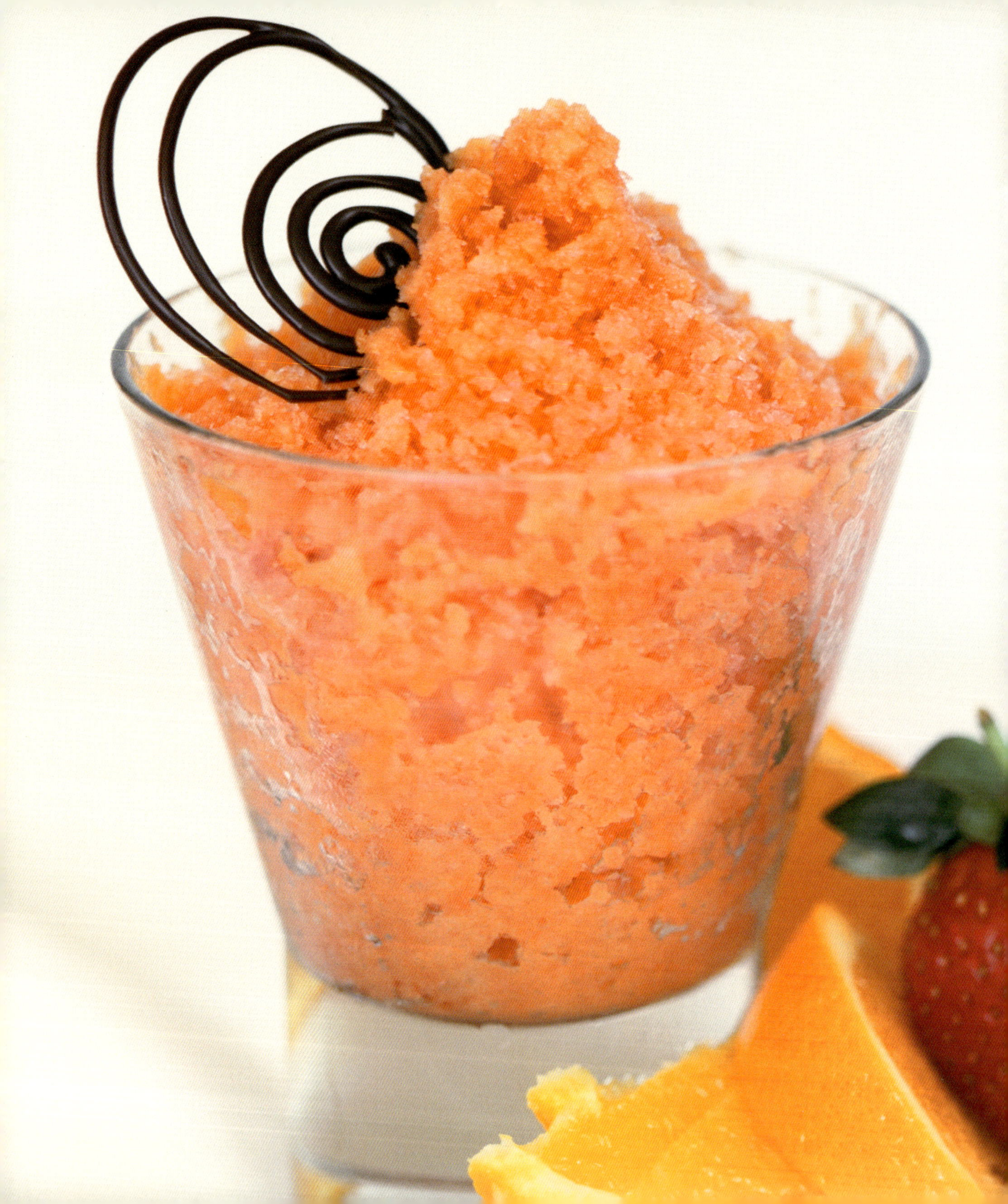

Tropical Grand Marnier Freeze

Makes approximately 500 ml (2 cups)

1 sachet gelatin
180 ml (¾ cup) boiling water
2 cups strawberries, chopped
4 oranges, peeled and diced
1 teaspoon castor sugar
90 ml (⅓ cup) Grand Marnier

Sprinkle gelatin over boiling water and stir until dissolved. Blend strawberries, oranges, sugar and Grand Marnier until smooth. Add the cooled gelatin mix and blend. Pour into a shallow baking dish or ice cube tray and freeze for ½ hour, or until almost frozen. Remove from freezer, place into blender and beat until fluffy. Re-freeze for a further two hours or until firm.

Alternatively place all chilled ingredients into ice-cream machine and leave to churn and freeze. Decorate with strawberries to serve.

Cointreau and Strawberry Sorbet

Makes approximately 500 ml (2 cups)

2 punnets strawberries
45 ml (1½ fl oz) Cointreau
30 ml (1 fl oz) strawberry liqueur
1 tablespoon castor sugar
8 ice cubes

Place all ingredients except ice cubes in blender, blend until smooth. Keeping blender running, add ice cubes one at a time, and continue blending until mixture is smooth. Pour into ice-cream tray and freeze.

Alternatively place all chilled ingredients into ice-cream machine and leave to churn and freeze.

To serve, allow to soften slightly, place in parfait glasses and garnish with mint and strawberries.

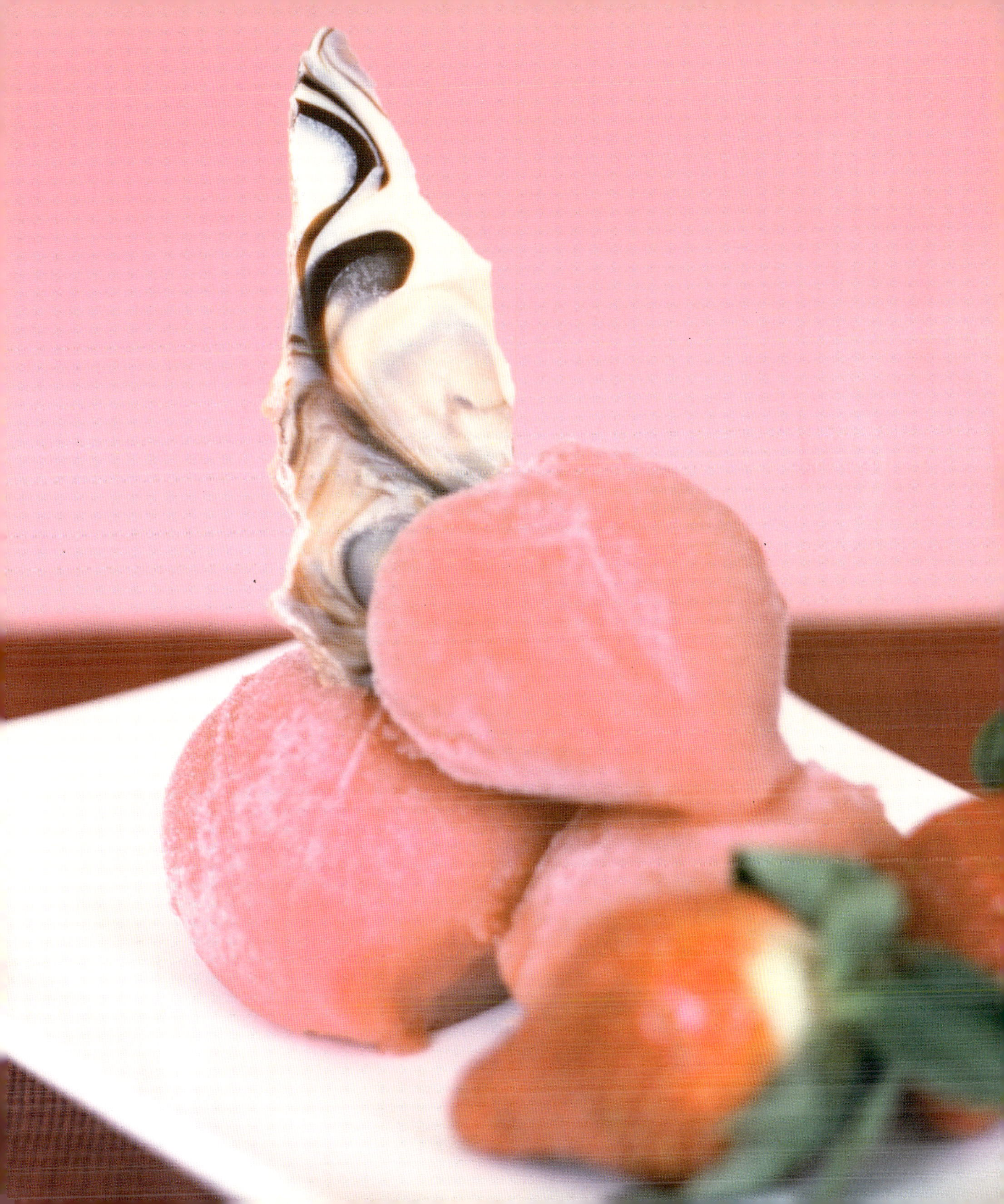

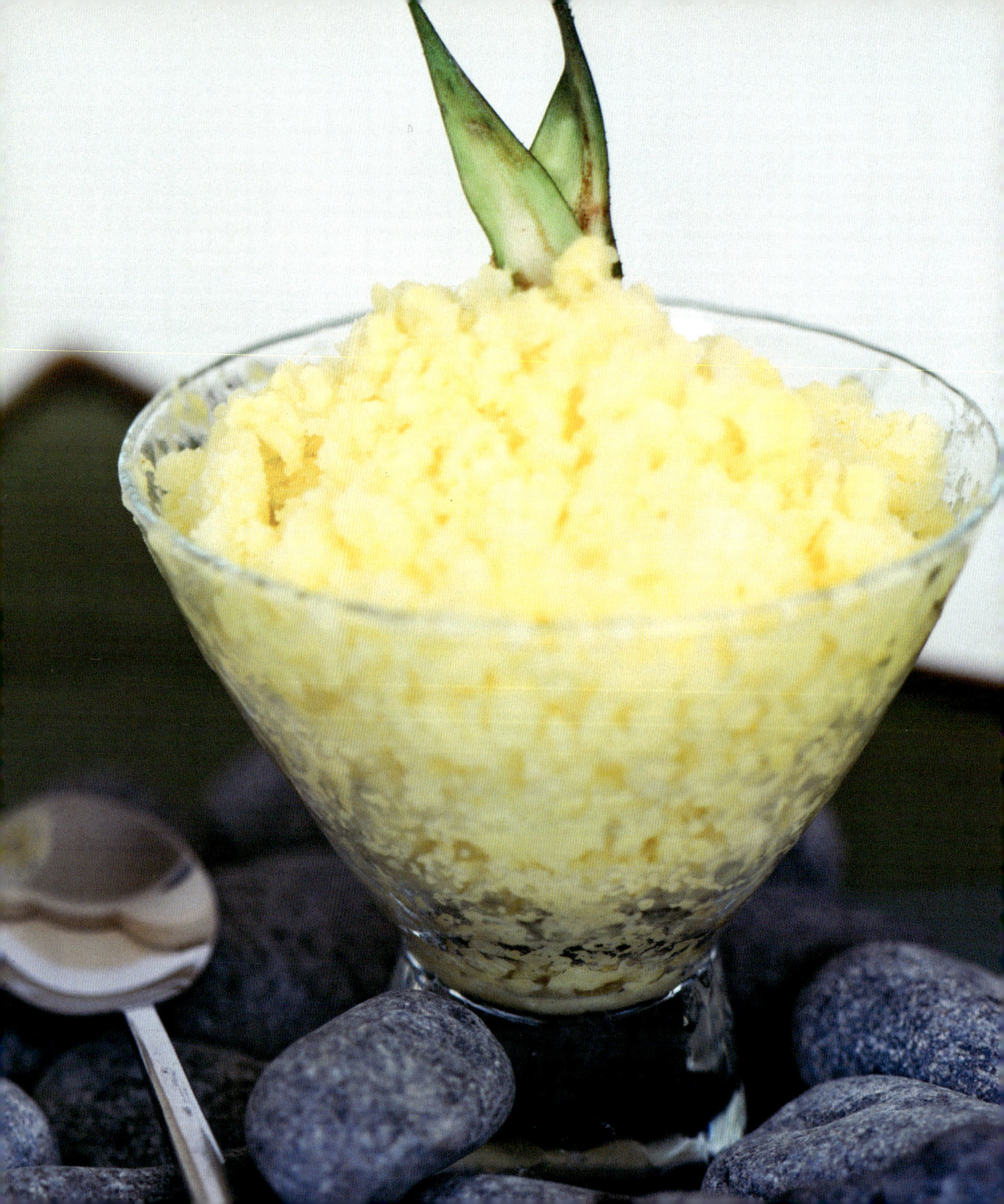

Pina Colada Sorbet

Makes approximately 500 ml (2 cups)

½ pineapple skinned, cored and diced
75 ml (2½ fl oz) Bacardi
15 ml (½ fl oz) Malibu
30 ml (1 fl oz) coconut cream
2 teaspoons desiccated coconut
2 tablespoons castor sugar
8 ice cubes

Place all ingredients except ice cubes in blender, blend until smooth. Keeping blender running, add ice cubes one at a time, and continue blending until mixture is smooth. Pour into ice-cream tray and freeze.

Alternatively place all chilled ingredients into ice-cream machine and leave to churn and freeze.

To serve, allow to soften slightly, place in parfait glasses and garnish with mint.

Strawberry and Lychee Cream Freeze

Makes approximately 750 ml (3 cups)

1 sachet gelatin
60 ml (¼ cup) boiling water
2 eggs, separated
60 g (2 oz) castor sugar
250 ml (1 cup) cream
45 ml (1½ fl oz) strawberry liqueur
45 ml (1½ fl oz) Paraiso lychee liqueur
1 punnet strawberries, washed and halved, stems removed
1 x 400 g (12 oz) can halved lychees, discard juice

Stir gelatin into boiling water until gelatin has dissolved, allow to cool. Combine egg yolks and sugar and beat until thick and white. Add cooled gelatin mix, beating until well combined.

In a separate bowl lightly beat the cream. Add the egg/gelatin mix and alcohol and stir well.

Whip the egg whites until stiff peaks form then fold into the mixture. Add halved strawberries and lychees to the mixture and fold through.

Pour mixture into a flat, high-sided tray and place in freezer for three to four hours. Once frozen cut into squares and serve.

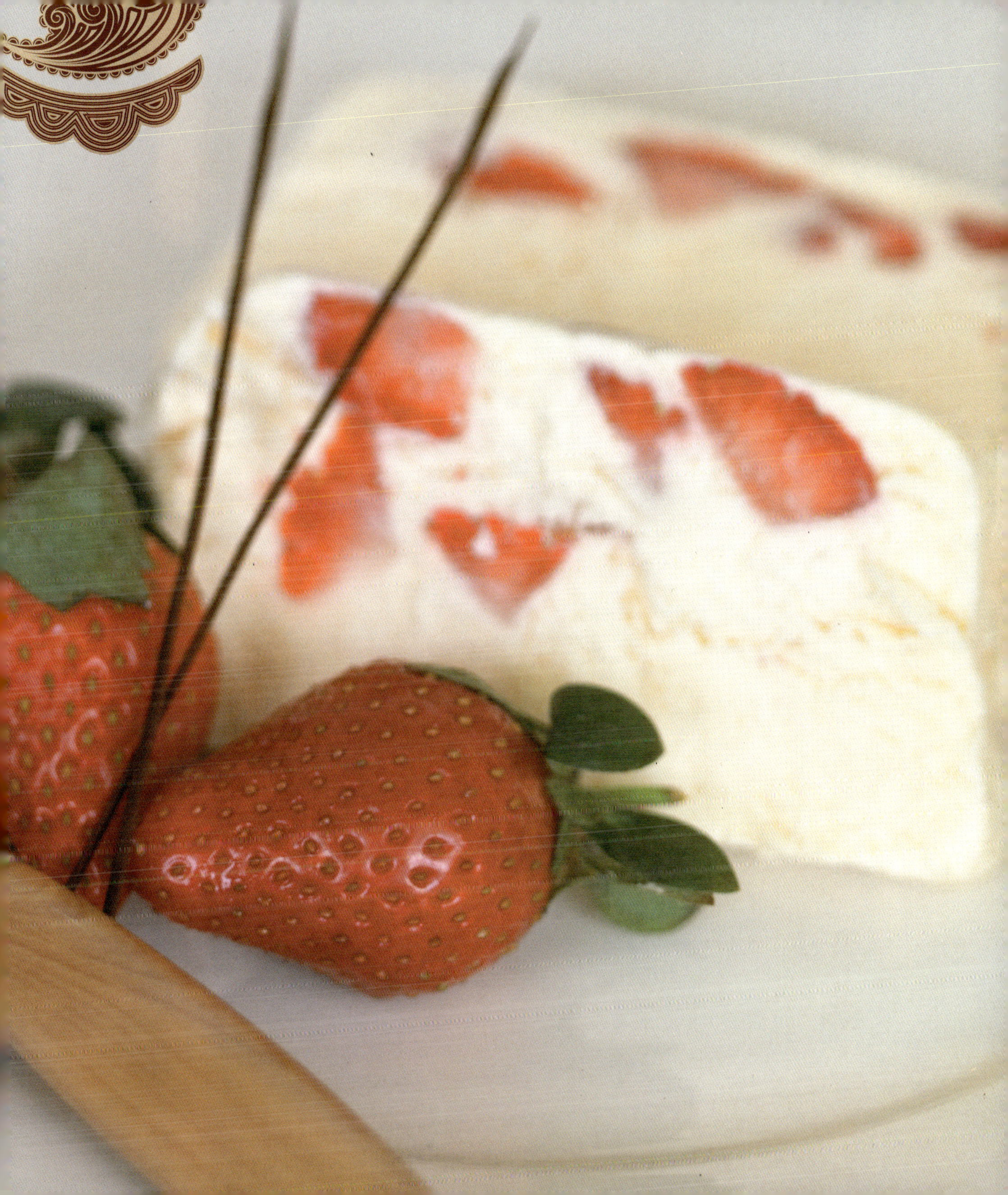

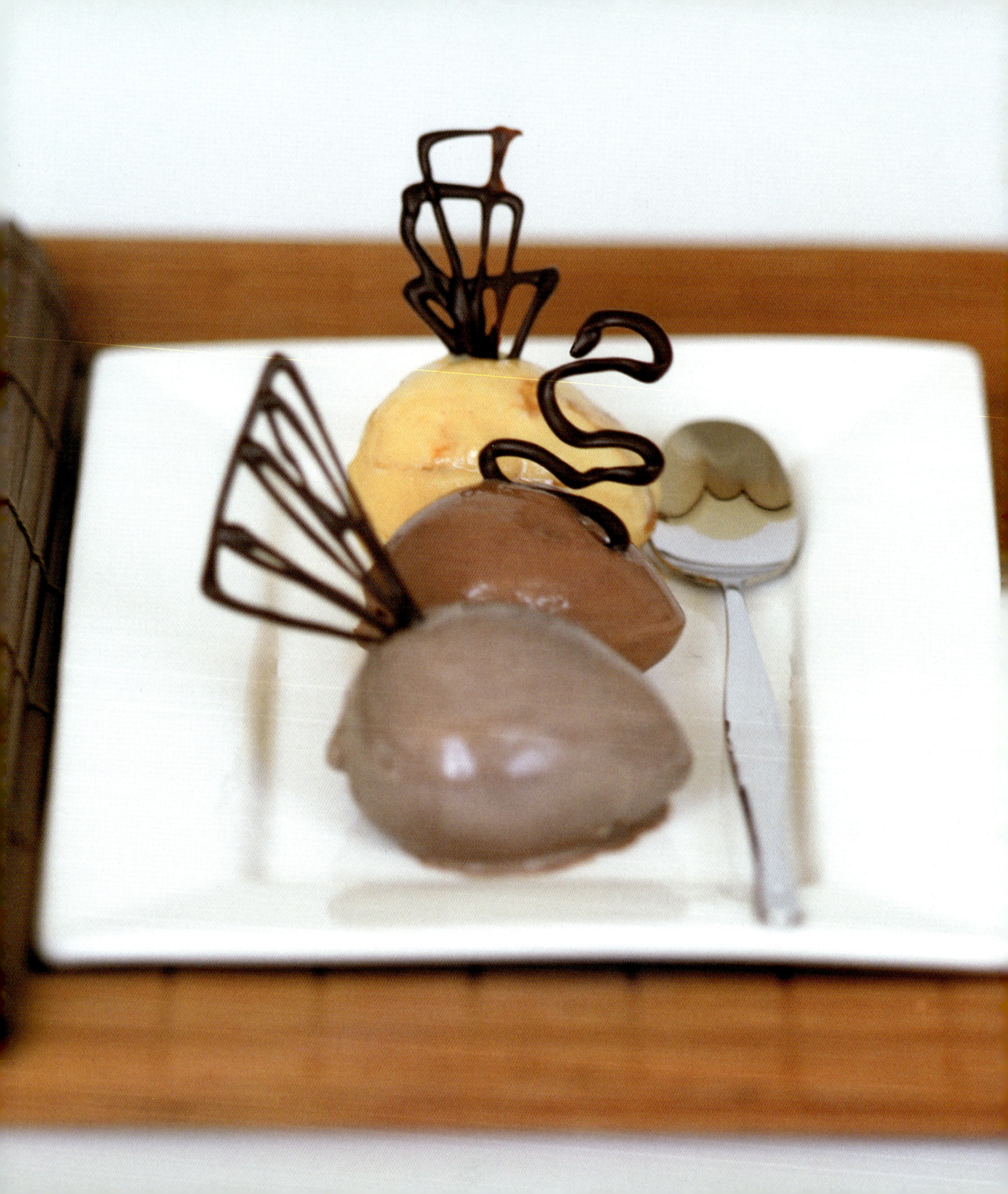

Creamy Chocolate Ice-cream

Makes approximately 750 ml (3 cups)

Note: This recipe works best with an ice-cream machine.

120 g (4 oz) chocolate bits
125 ml (½ cup) castor sugar
250 ml (1 cup) milk
2 egg yolks
150 ml (2/3 cup) cream
100 ml (3½ fl oz) Crème de Cacao

Place chocolate, sugar and half the milk in a saucepan and heat gently until chocolate melts. Combine remaining milk and egg yolks then add to the chocolate mixture. Bring mixture gently to the boil, stirring constantly. Remove from the heat and allow to cool. The mixture will resemble custard. Refrigerate overnight.

The following day add cream and Crème de Cacao and mix with a wire whisk. Pour chilled mixture into ice-cream machine and leave to churn and freeze.

Creamy Baileys Irish Cream Ice-cream

Makes approximately 750 ml (3 cups)

Note: This recipe works best with an ice-cream machine.

125 ml (½ cup) castor sugar
200 ml (7 fl oz) milk
2 egg yolks
250 ml (1 cup) cream
150 ml (2/3 cup) Baileys Irish Cream

Place sugar and half the milk in a saucepan and heat gently until sugar dissolves. Combine remaining milk and egg yolks then add to the hot mixture. Bring mixture gently to the boil, stirring constantly. Remove from the heat and allow to cool. The mixture will resemble custard. Refrigerate overnight.

The following day, add cream and Baileys, mix with a wire whisk. Pour chilled mixture into an ice-cream machine and leave to churn and freeze.

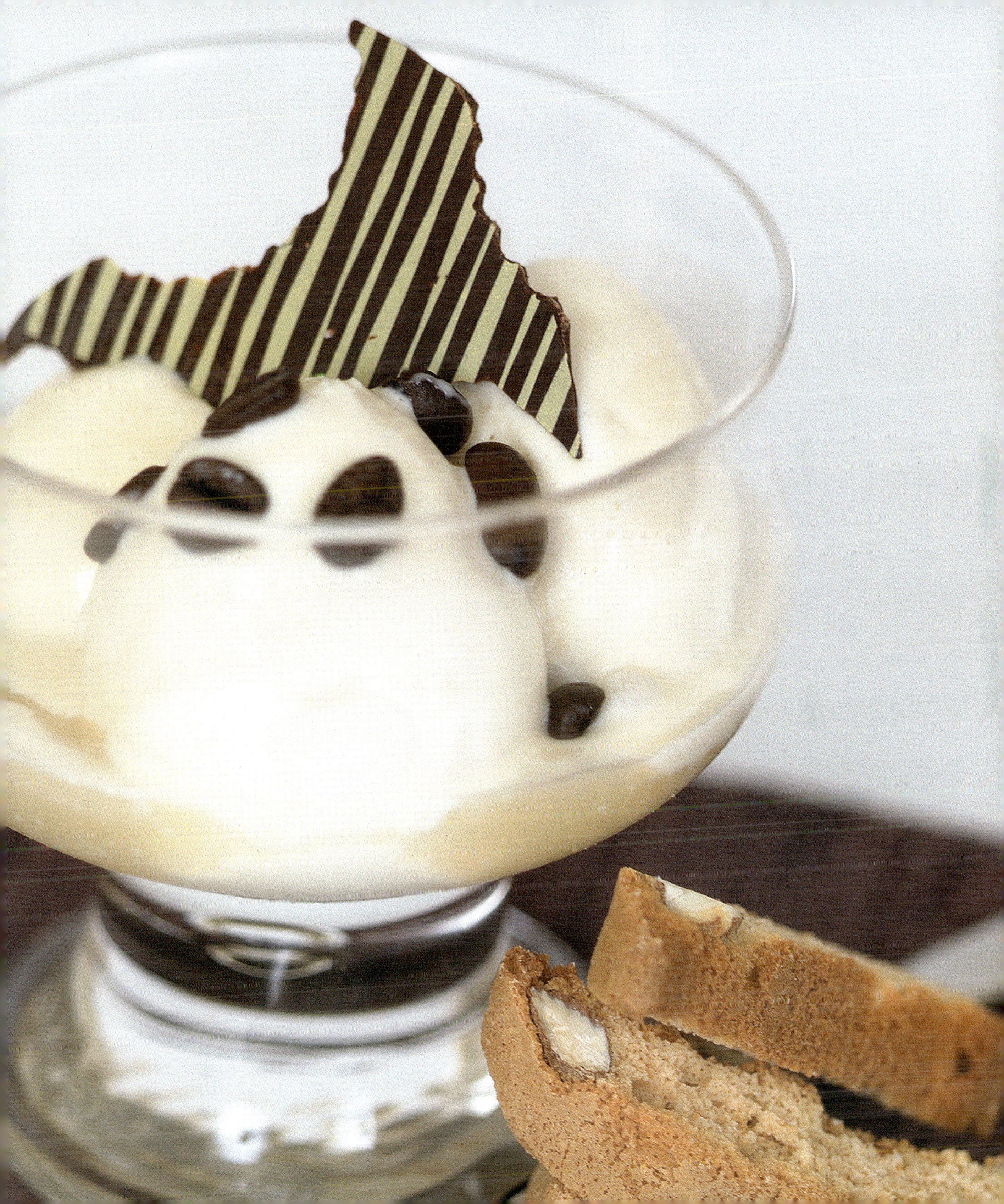

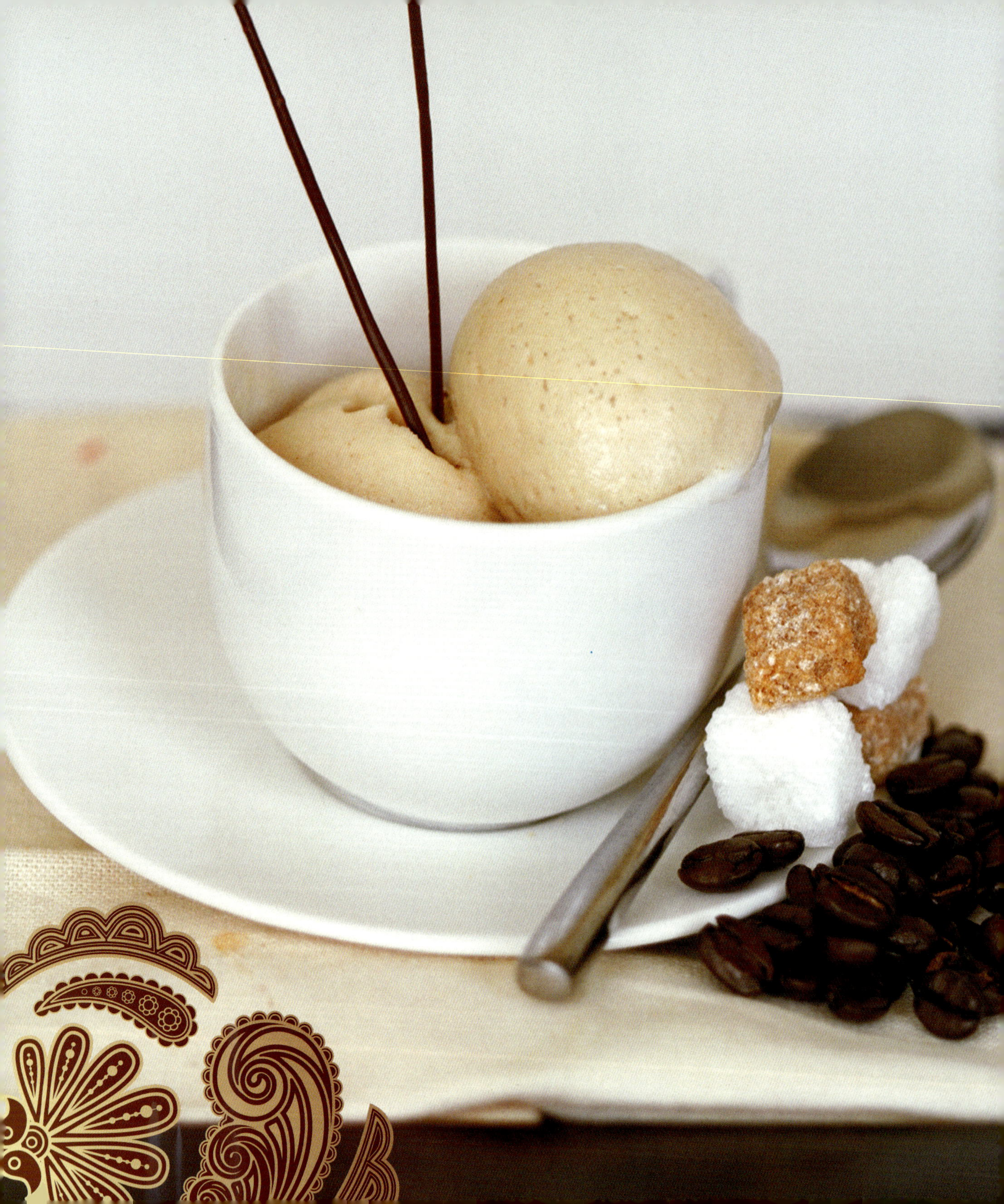

Baileys Irish Cream and Coffee Ice-cream

Makes approximately 750 ml (3 cups)

Note: This recipe works best with an ice-cream machine.

125 ml (½ cup) percolated coffee
125 g (½ cup) castor sugar
100 g (3½ oz) chocolate
125 ml (½ cup) milk
2 egg yolks
200 ml (7 fl oz) cream
90 ml (⅓ cup) Baileys Irish Cream
60 ml (¼ cup) Crème de Cacao

Place the coffee, sugar and chocolate into a saucepan and simmer gently for about three minutes until the sugar and chocolate have dissolved. In a separate bowl whisk the milk with the egg yolks, add to the mix in the saucepan and bring gently to the boil. Place mixture in the refrigerator to cool, preferably overnight.

Stir in the cream and the alcohol. Place all chilled ingredients into an ice-cream machine and leave to churn and freeze.

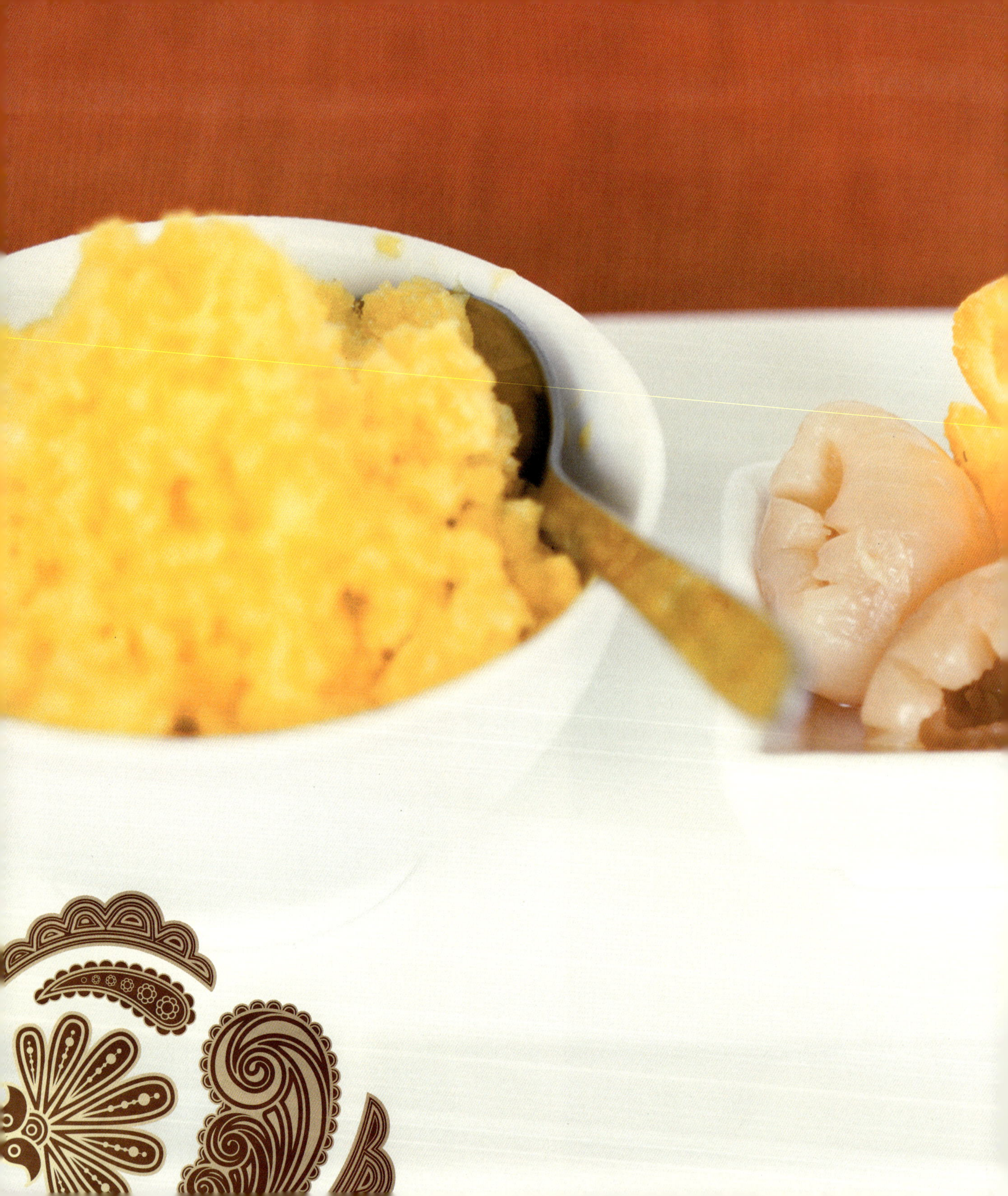

Orange and Lychee Daiquiri Bomb

Makes approximately 750 ml (3 cups)

8 medium oranges
1 x 400 g (13 oz) can lychees (reserve syrup)
60 g (2 oz) castor sugar
60 ml (¼ cup) Paraiso lychee liqueur
90 ml (⅓ cup) Bacardi
16 ice cubes

Cut the tops off the oranges neatly (keep the tops) and hollow out. Place orange pulp in a blender with lychees, lychee syrup, sugar and liqueur and blend well. Add ice cubes several at a time and blend. Once all ingredients are blended pour mix in ice-cream machine and churn until almost frozen, then scoop mixture into the orange shells and place in the freezer with the tops on as lids. Leave to freeze overnight. Remove from the freezer several minutes prior to serving.

Note: These bombs can be served in a martini glass instead of in the oranges.

Creamy Banana Ice-cream

Makes approximately 750 ml (3 cups)

Note: This recipe works best with an ice-cream machine.

5 medium bananas
3 egg yolks
180 g (6 oz) castor sugar
350 ml (11 fl oz) cream
100 ml (3½ fl oz) banana liqueur
100 ml (3½ fl oz) milk

Place all ingredients in a blender or food processor and process until smooth. Pour chilled, blended ingredients into an ice-cream machine and leave to churn and freeze.

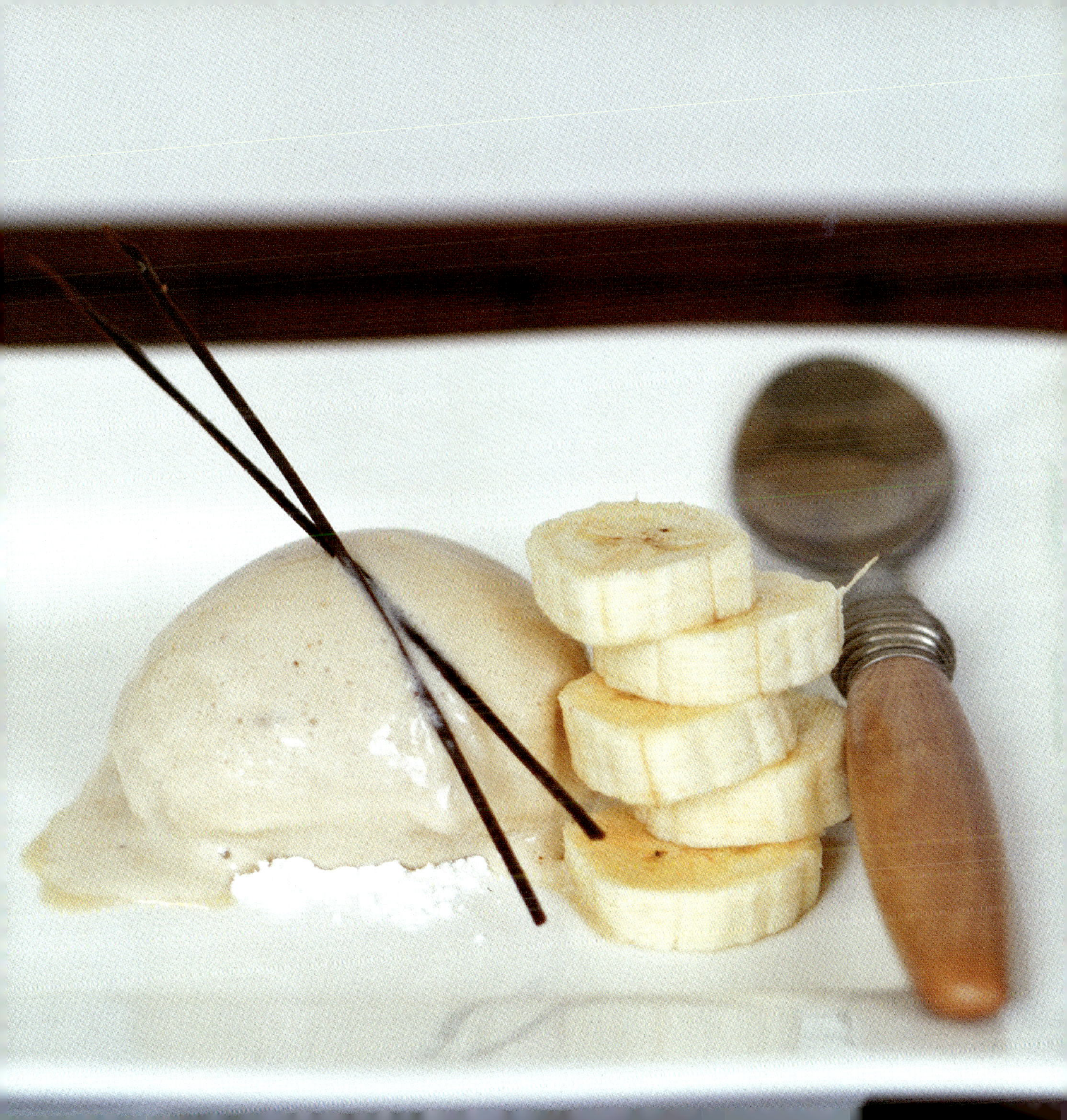

Creamy Strawberry Ice-cream

Makes approximately 750 ml (3 cups)

250 g (8 oz) fresh strawberries, washed and cut
3 egg yolks
180 g (6 oz) castor sugar
350 ml (1¼ cups) cream
100 ml (3½ fl oz) strawberry liqueur
100 ml (3½ fl oz) milk

Place all ingredients in a blender or food processor and process until smooth. Pour chilled, blended ingredients into an ice-cream machine and leave to churn and freeze.

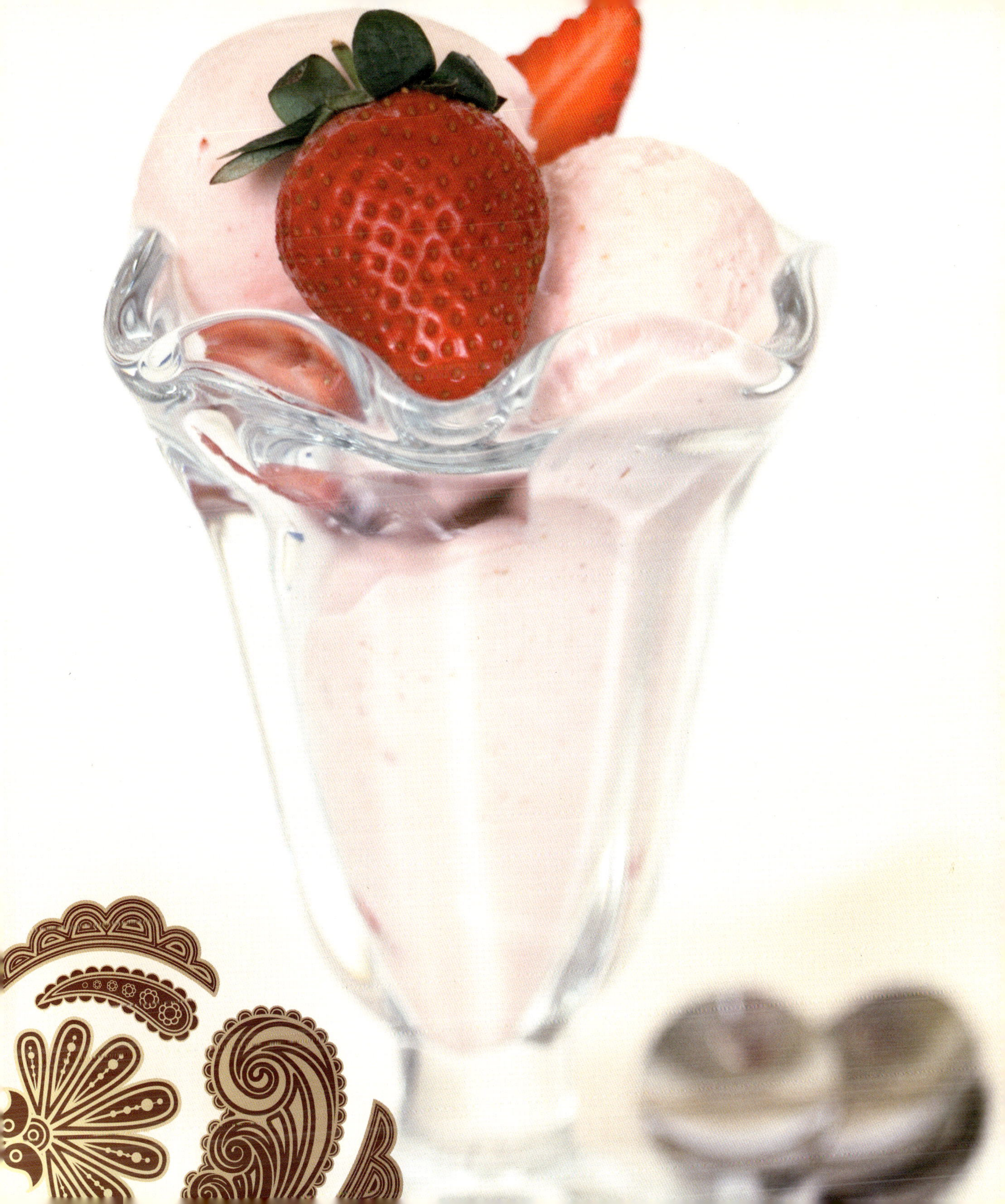

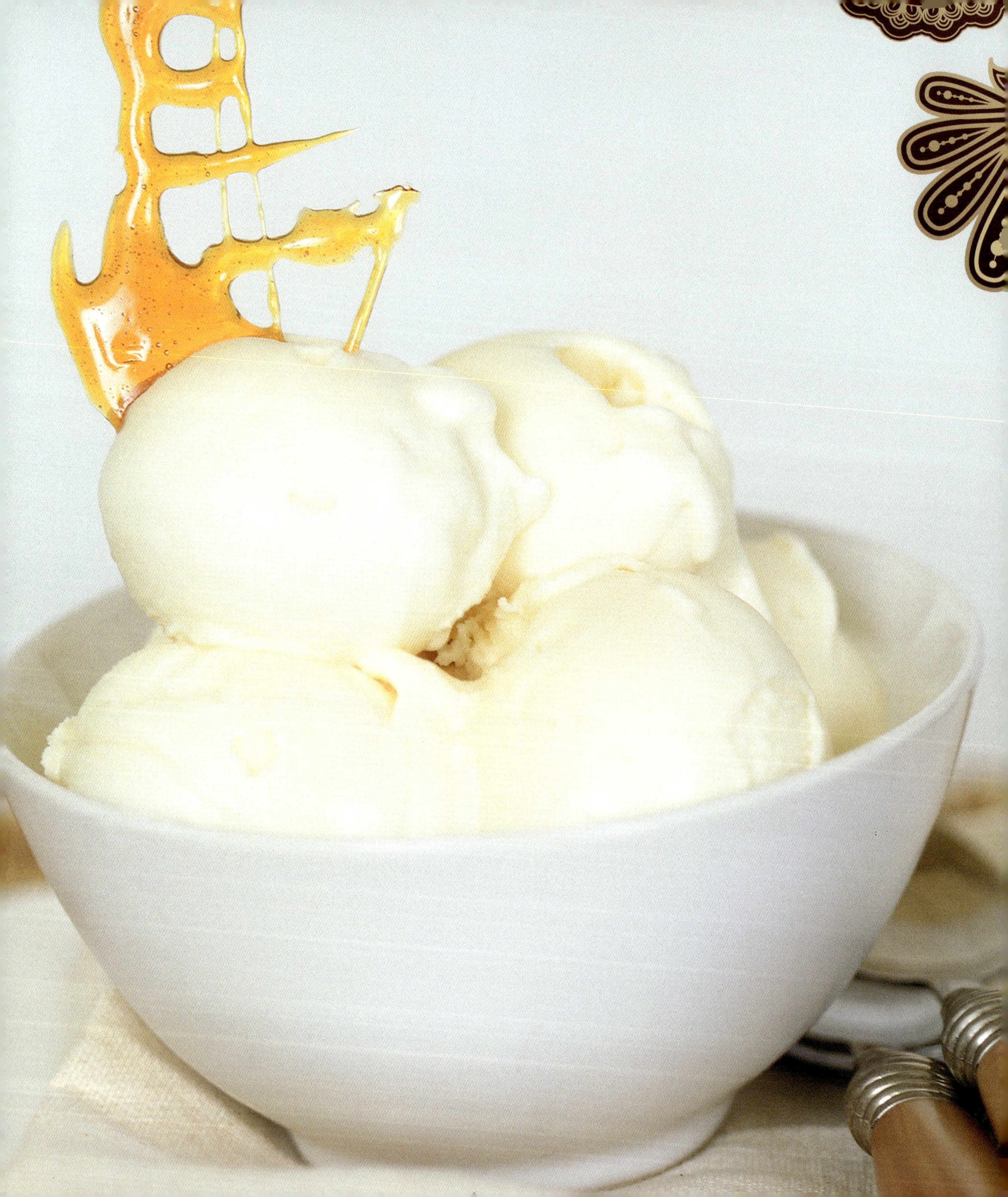

Creamy Butterscotch Ice-cream

Note: This recipe works best with an ice-cream machine.

125 ml (½ cup) castor sugar
250 ml (1 cup) milk
2 egg yolks
75 ml (⅓ cup) Baileys Irish Cream
75 ml (⅓ cup) butterscotch liqueur or butterscotch schnapps
250 ml (1 cup) cream

Makes approximately 750 ml (3 cups)

Place sugar and half the milk in a saucepan and heat gently until sugar dissolves. Combine remaining milk and egg yolks then add to the hot mixture. Bring mixture gently to the boil, stirring constantly. Remove from the heat and allow cooling. The mixture will resemble custard. Refrigerate overnight.

The following day, add cream and liqueurs, mix with a wire whisk. Pour chilled mixture into ice-cream machine and leave to churn and freeze.

Midori and Honeydew Melon Sorbet

Makes approximately 500 ml (2 cups)

1 honeydew melon, cubed and skin and seeds removed
125 ml (½ cup) Midori
15 ml (½ fl oz) lemon juice
1 tablespoon castor sugar
8 ice cubes

Place all ingredients except ice cubes in blender, blend until smooth. Keeping blender running, add ice cubes one at a time, and continue blending until mixture is smooth. Pour into ice-cream tray and freeze. Alternatively place all chilled ingredients into an ice-cream machine and leave to churn and freeze.

To serve, allow to soften slightly then place in parfait glasses.

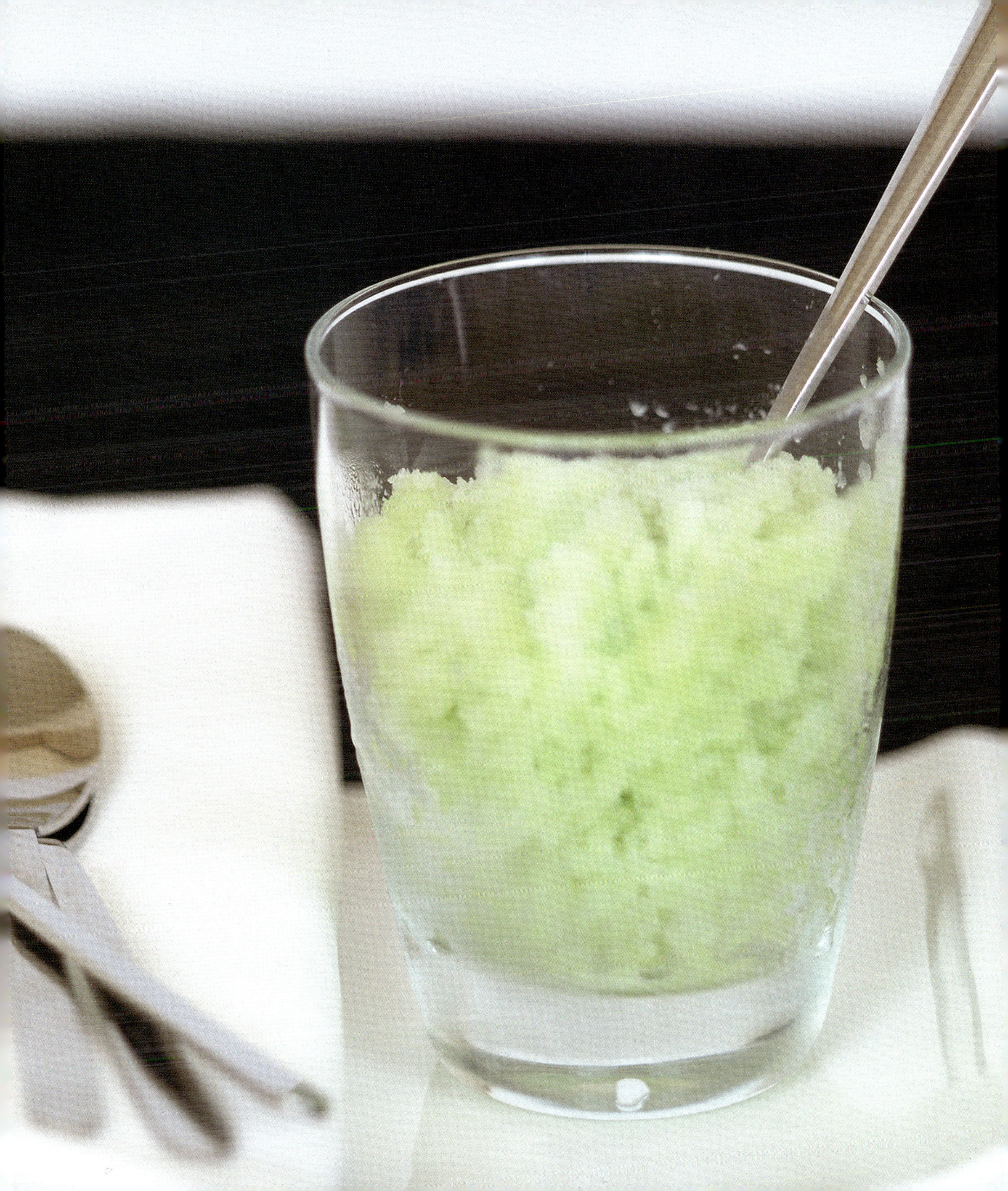

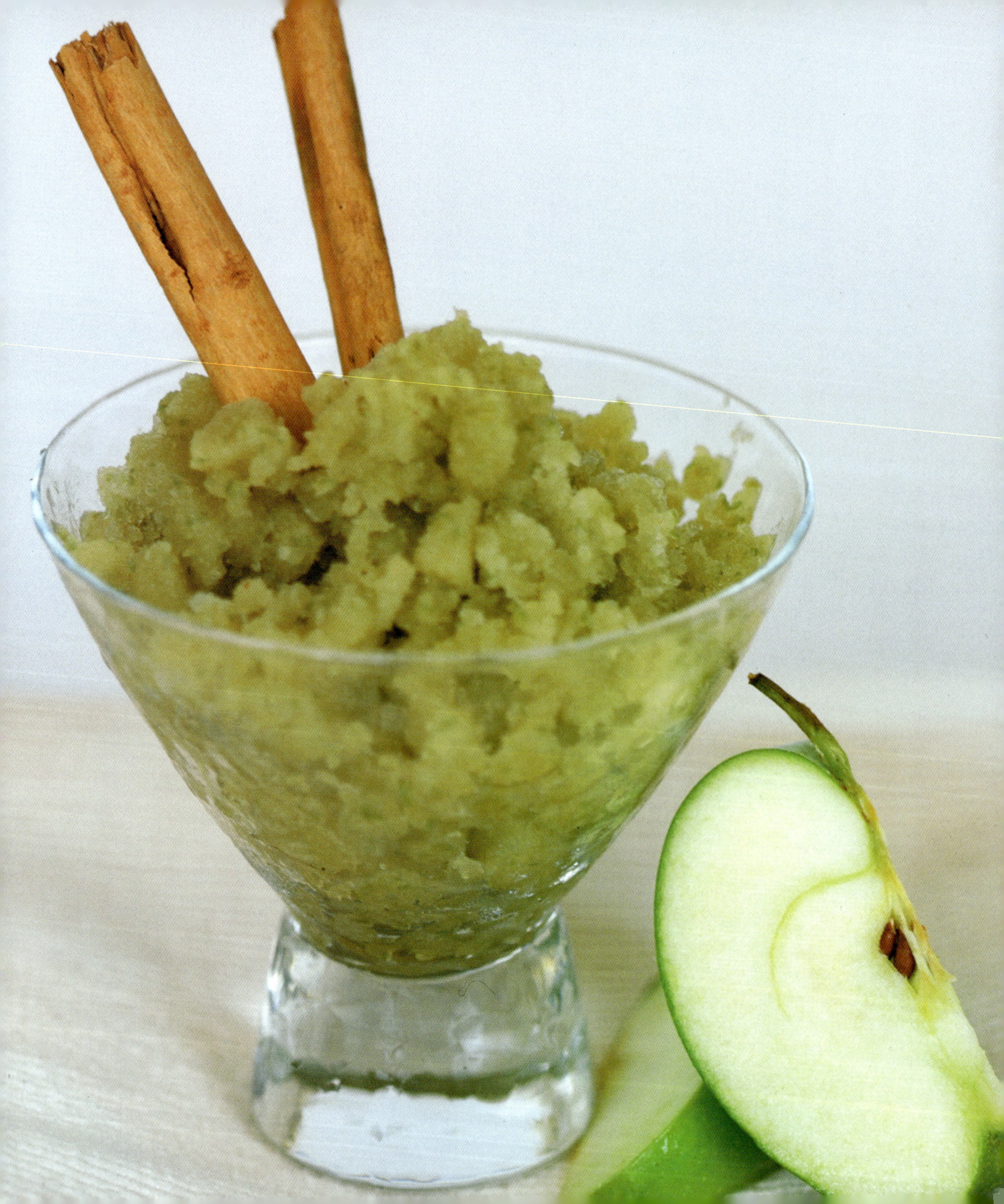

Apple Strudel Sorbet

Makes approximately 500 ml (2 cups)

60 ml (¼ cup) Frangelico
60 ml (¼ cup) apple schnapps
6 large or 8 medium green apples, cored and skin left on
15 ml (½ fl oz) lime juice
3 tablespoons brown sugar
½ teaspoon cinnamon
8 ice cubes

Place all ingredients except ice cubes in blender, blend until smooth. Keeping blender running, add ice cubes one at a time, and continue blending until mixture is smooth. Pour into ice-cream tray and freeze. Alternatively place all chilled ingredients into an ice-cream machine and leave to churn and freeze.

To serve, allow to soften slightly then place in parfait glasses.

Frangelico, Kiwi Fruit and Lime Sorbet

Makes approximately 500 ml (2 cups)

125 ml (½ cup) Frangelico
8 kiwi fruit, skinned
2 fresh limes, juiced with pulp
1 tablespoon castor sugar
12 ice cubes

Place all ingredients except ice cubes in blender, blend until smooth. Keeping blender running, add ice cubes one at a time, and continue blending until mixture is smooth. Pour into ice-cream tray and freeze. Alternatively place all chilled ingredients into ice-cream machine and leave to churn and freeze.

To serve, allow to soften slightly then place in parfait glasses.

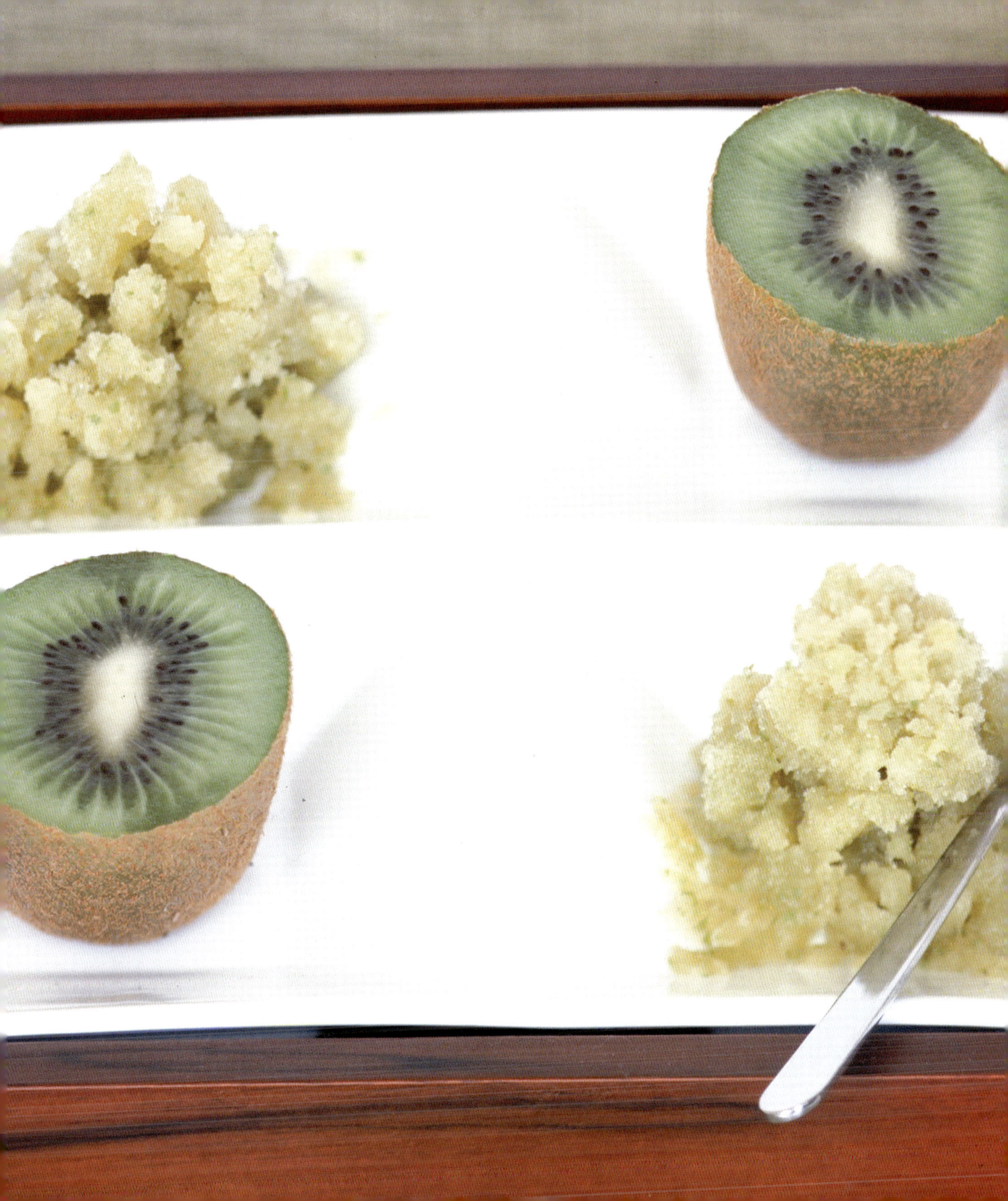

Cakes, tarts, puddings and trifles

A mouthwatering selection of hot and cold cakes and puddings to finish with a flourish.

Pear and Chambord Crumble

Serves 8

10 pears, core removed and skinned, cut in slivers
½ punnet blackberries, halved
½ punnet raspberries, halved
125 ml (½ cup) Chambord
125 g (4 oz) castor sugar

Topping
125 g (4 oz) flour
125 g (4 oz) brown sugar
125 g (4 oz) chilled butter
125 g (4 oz) rolled oats
125 g (4 oz) toasted muesli

Preheat oven to 180°C (360°F). Butter a large square or rectangular baking dish.

Layer fruits in baking dish and sprinkle with the castor sugar. Drizzle Chambord over fruit. Allow to soak in Chambord for at least a couple of hours.

To make topping: In a blender, combine the flour, brown sugar and butter until crumbly. Pour into bowl and mix in oats and muesli.

Crumble the topping over the fruits and bake in preheated oven for 45 minutes until the crumble is bubbling and golden on top.

Remove from oven and allow to cool slightly. Serve warm with ice-cream or fresh cream.

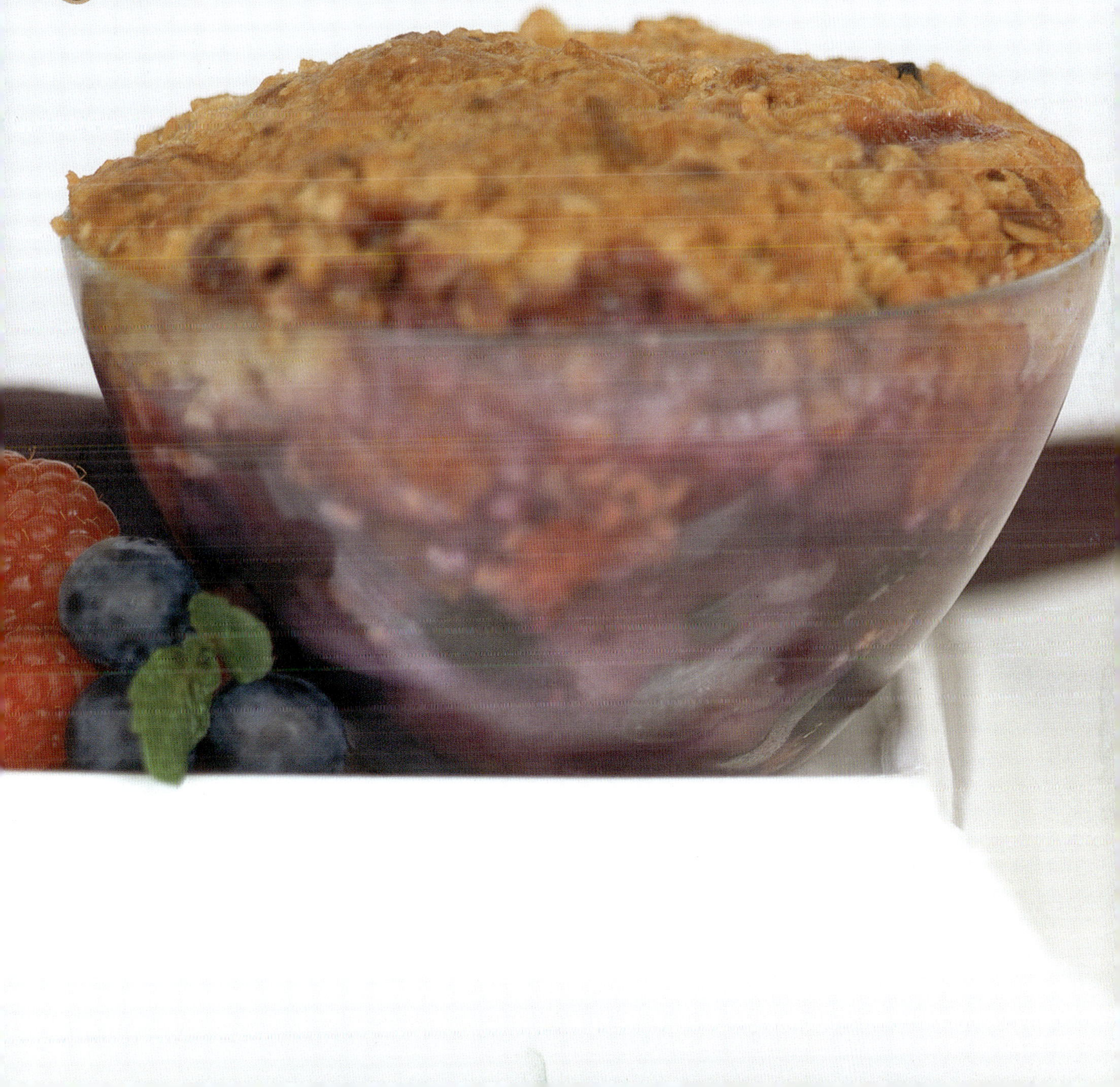

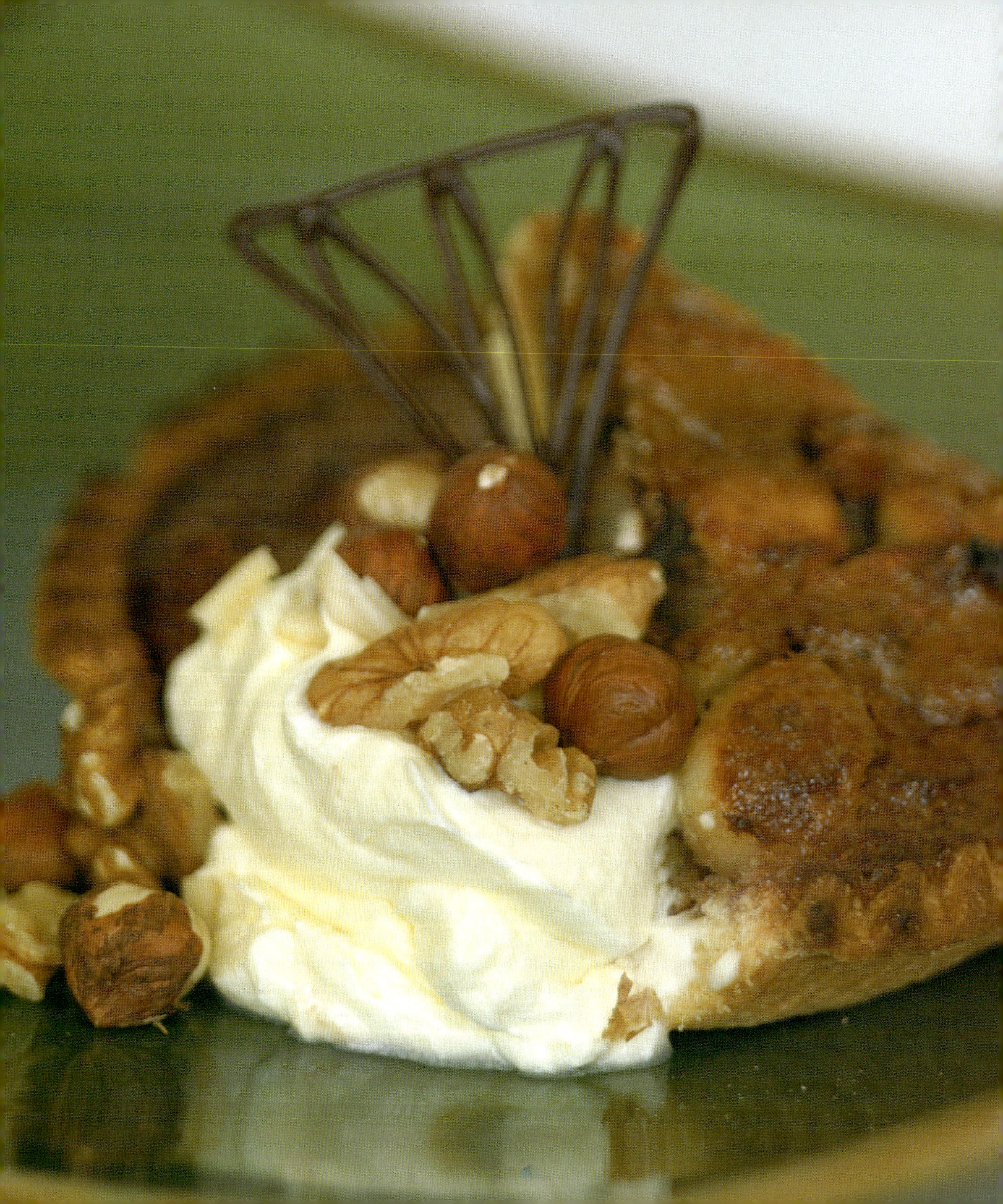

Macadamia and Hazelnut Tart

Serves 10

1 large (or 2 small) sweet pastry shell
170 g (5½ oz) brown sugar
250 ml (1 cup) golden syrup
60 g butter
300 g (10 oz) raw macadamias and hazelnuts
2 eggs, beaten with 2 tablespoons water
90 ml (⅓ cup) Frangelico
60 g (2 oz) white breadcrumbs

Melt the brown sugar, golden syrup and butter over a low heat, do not boil. Allow to cool.

Pulse nuts in food processor until a coarse texture. Stir eggs and Frangelico into sugar mixture, then the nuts and finally the breadcrumbs. Pour mixture into shell. Bake at 180°C (350°F) for approximately 25 minutes until golden and set.

Tia Maria Log

Serves 8

250 ml (1 cup) cream
1 tablespoon icing sugar
90 ml (⅓ cup) **Tia Maria**
250 g (8 oz) **packet chocolate biscuits**
125 ml (½ cup) grated chocolate

Beat cream and icing sugar until slightly thickened, lightly beat in Tia Maria. Layer mixture and biscuits until all biscuits are used, creating a log. Coat log in remaining cream mixture then roll log in grated chocolate. Refrigerate prior to serving.

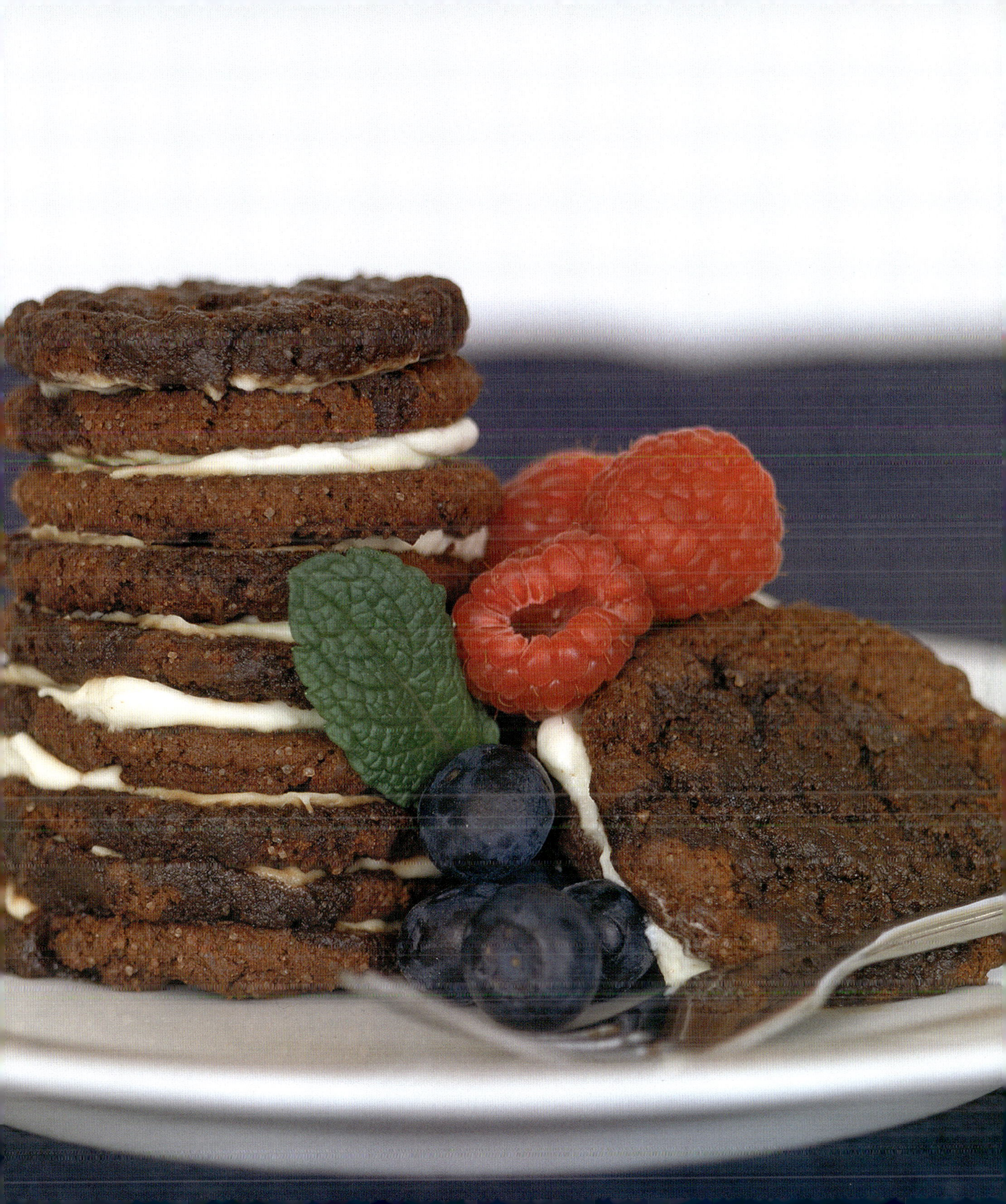

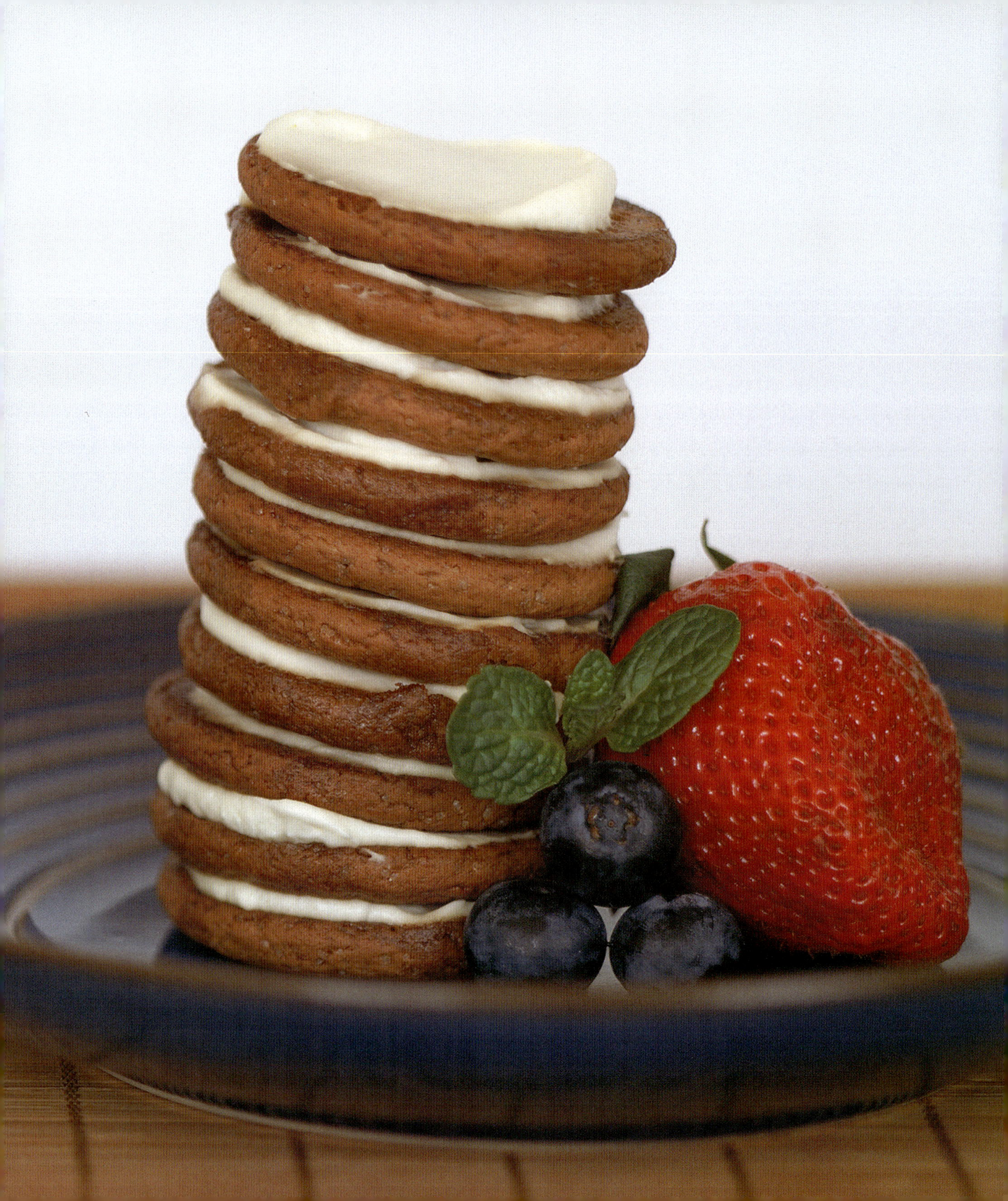

Ginger Log

Serves 8

250 ml (1 cup) cream
1 tablespoon icing sugar
90 ml (⅓ cup) liqueur (such as Kahlua, Tia Maria, Cointreau or Frangelico)
250 g (8 oz) ginger biscuits
125 ml (½ cup) grated chocolate

Beat cream and icing sugar until slightly thickened, lightly beat in liqueur. Layer mixture and biscuits until all biscuits are used, creating a log. Coat log in remaining cream mixture then roll log in grated chocolate. Refrigerate prior to serving.

Pavlova with Chocolate Cream

Serves 10

Meringue
8 egg whites (at room temperature)
500g (2 cups) castor sugar
1 tablespoon vinegar
½ teaspoon vanilla

Cream
250 ml (1 cup) cream
1 tablespoon icing sugar
60 ml (¼ cup) Crème de Cacao
1 banana, sliced

To make meringue: Beat egg whites until peaks form. Add sugar slowly and beat well, then add vinegar and vanilla. Mixture should be glossy.

Grease baking tray and line with wet, brown paper bag. Pile mixture onto bag and shake gently. Bake at 150°C (300°F) for 1½ to 2 hours.

Once cooked, carefully remove meringue from the oven. The brown paper bag will easily peel off the base. Place meringue onto a serving plate.

To make cream: Beat cream and icing sugar until thick, add Crème de Cacao and continue beating until thick. Top with sliced banana.

Pavlova with Cointreau Cream

Serves 10

Meringue
8 egg whites (at room temperature)
500 g (2 cups) castor sugar
1 tablespoon vinegar
½ teaspoon vanilla

Cream
250 ml (1 cup) cream
1 tablespoon icing sugar
60 ml (¼ cup) Cointreau

Fresh season fruit, chopped, to garnish (such as strawberries, kiwi fruit, berries)

To make meringue: Beat egg whites until peaks form. Add sugar slowly and beat well, then add vinegar and vanilla. Mixture should be glossy.

Grease baking tray and line with wet, brown paper bag. Pile mixture onto bag and shake gently. Bake at 150°C (300°F) for 1½ to 2 hours.

Once cooked carefully remove meringue from the oven. The brown paper bag will easily peel off the base. Place meringue onto a serving plate.

To make cream: Beat cream and icing sugar until thick, add Cointreau and continue beating until thick. Top with selected fruits.

Chocolate Bread and Butter Pudding

Serves 10

8 slices fruit loaf or brioche
70 g (2½ oz) butter
125 ml (½ cup) milk
450 ml (2 cups) thickened cream
125 ml (½ cup) castor sugar
1 x 100 g (3½ oz) Toblerone chocolate bar
4 eggs, lightly beaten
60 ml (¼ cup) Frangelico
60 ml (¼ cup) Crème de Cacao
125 ml (½ cup) grated or finely chopped chocolate
2 tablespoons golden syrup

Preheat oven to 180°C (350°F). Grease a large ovenproof baking dish. Butter fruit loaf or brioche and cut into triangles. Place bread on the base of the baking dish in layers.

In a large saucepan, combine milk, cream and sugar and stir well until the sugar dissolves. Bring this mixture to the boil then remove from heat. Add the chocolate and stir to combine. Allow this mixture to sit for ten minutes until the chocolate has totally melted. Stir well.

Add the lightly beaten eggs, and the Frangelico and Crème de Cacao and mix well to combine. Pour half the chocolate custard mixture over the bread and allow the bread to absorb the liquid before pouring over the remaining custard.

Sprinkle with chopped or grated chocolate and drizzle with golden syrup. Bake at 180°C (350°F) for 45 minutes or until the pudding looks puffy and is golden brown and firm to the touch. Sprinkle with icing sugar or cocoa if desired.

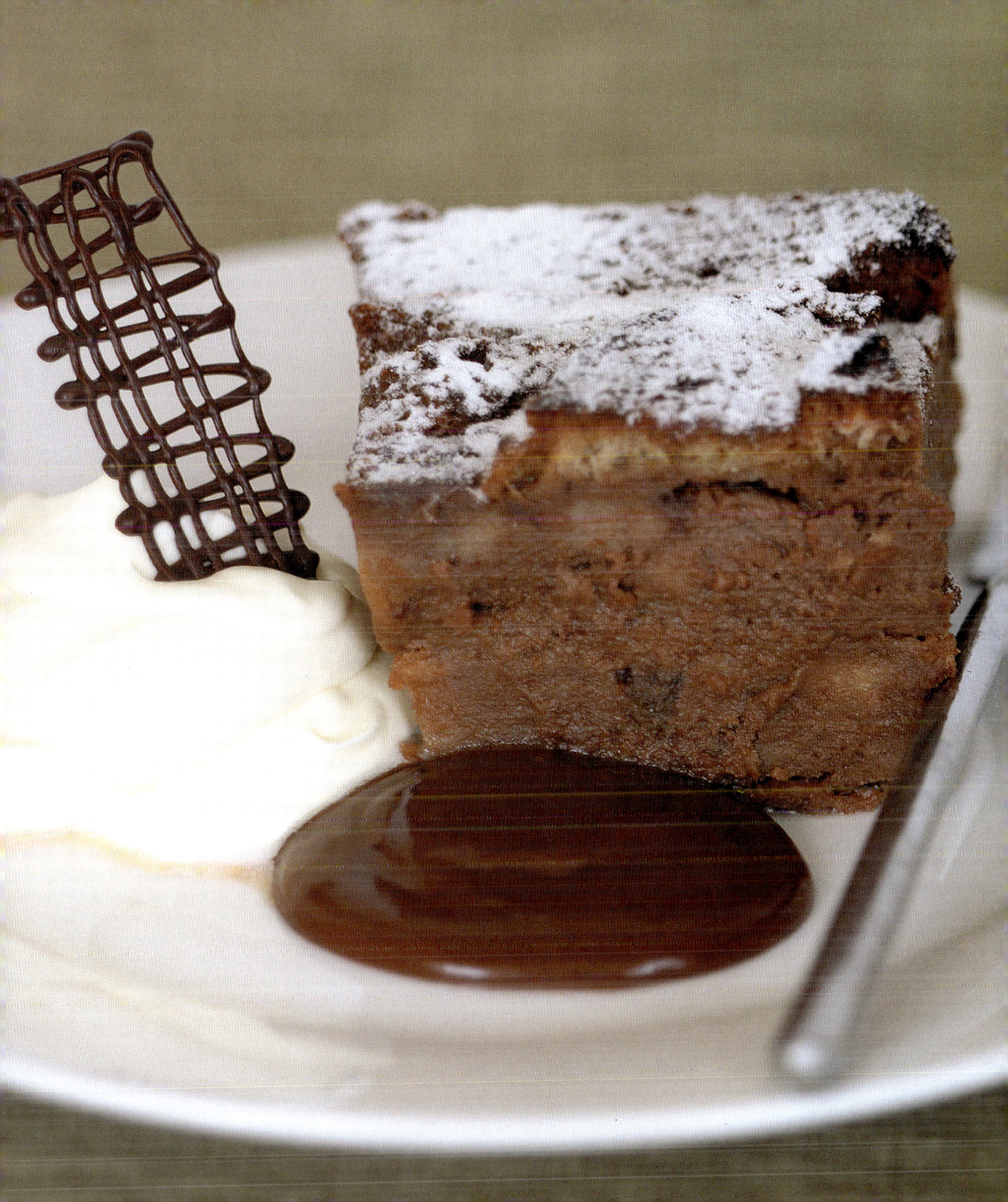

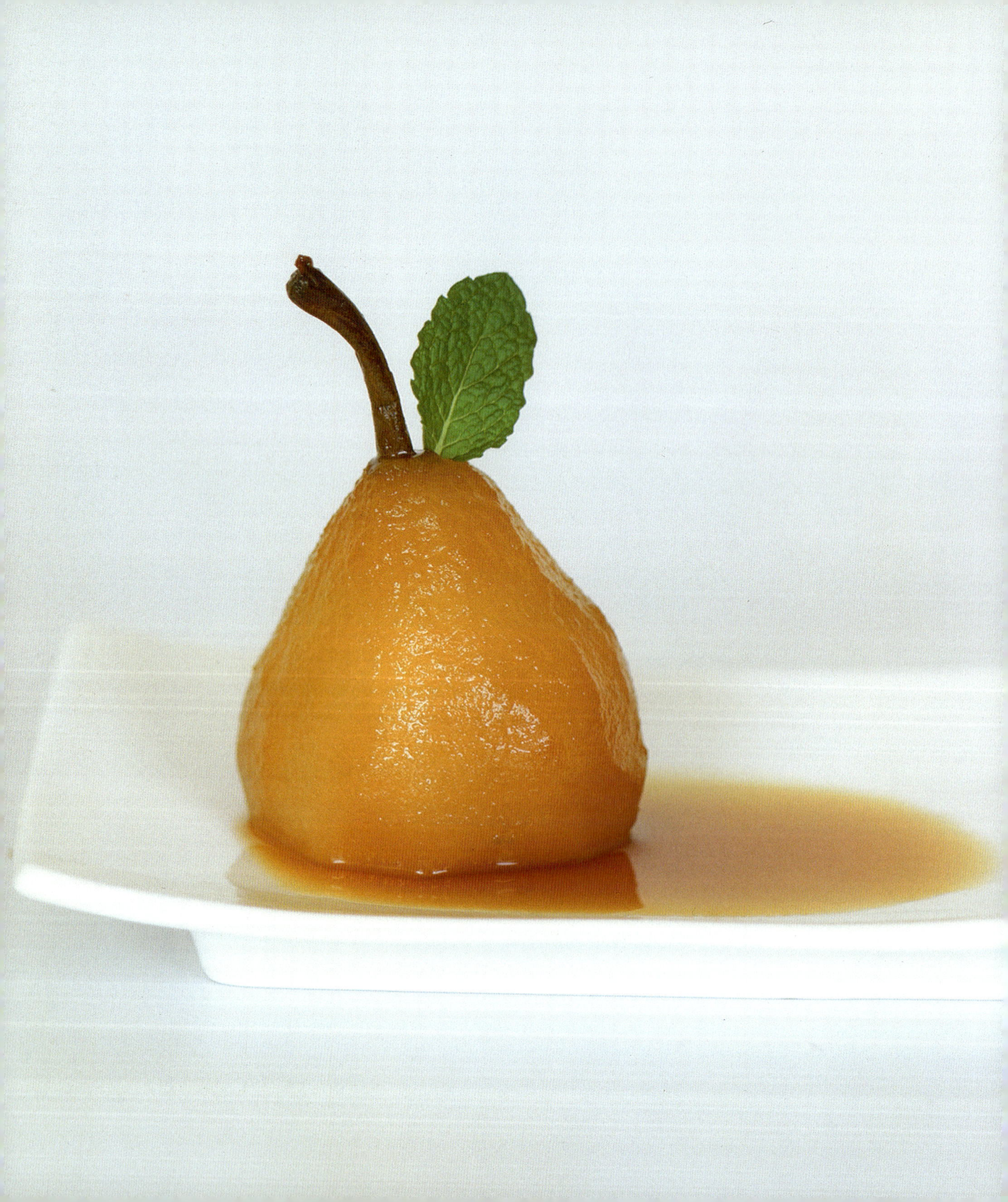

Poached Pears in Sweet White Wine

Serves 8

4 firm-ripe pears, whole and peeled but with stems intact
750 ml (3 cups) sweet white wine
180 g (6 oz) castor sugar
60 g (2 oz) brown sugar
Juice and zest of 1 lemon

Place the pears in a large saucepan then pour over the white wine, sugar and lemon. (Don't be concerned if the liquid does not cover the pears; when it starts to boil it rises.) Boil rapidly in the wine mixture until the pears are almost tender, about 20 minutes. Be careful that the wine does not reduce to the point where it starts to burn.

Serve the pears warm or cool, with fresh clotted or thickened cream.

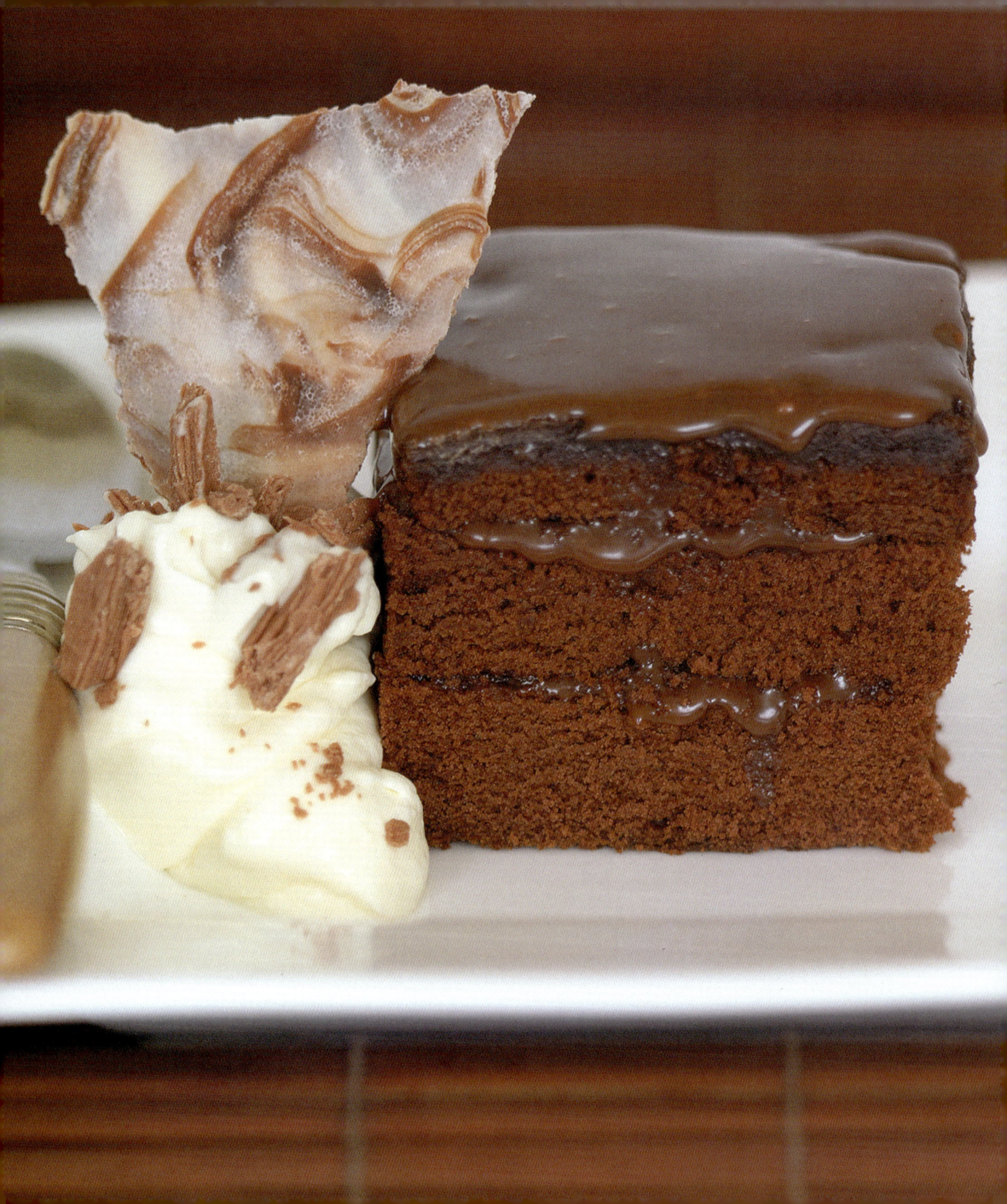

Chocolate Gateau

Serves 10

Cake
125 g (4 oz) butter
250 g (1 cup) self-raising flour
250 g (1 cup) castor sugar
60 g (2 oz) milk
60 g (2 oz) Crème de Cacao
½ teaspoon vanilla essence
2 eggs
2 heaped tablespoons cocoa
60 ml (¼ cup) Tia Maria to drizzle over cake

Ganache filling
60 ml (¼ cup) cream
40 ml (1½ fl oz) Tia Maria
125 g (4 oz) dark chocolate bits

Ganache topping
140 ml (2/3 cup) cream
60 ml (¼ cup) Tia Maria
250 g (8 oz) dark chocolate bits

To make cake: Prepare a well-buttered 20-cm (8-in) cake tin. Preheat oven to 180°C (350°F). Melt the butter then place with all other ingredients into a bowl and beat with electric beaters for approximately three to four minutes until well beaten. Pour into the cake tin.

Bake for approximately 50 minutes. Once cooked, cut the cake evenly through the middle and drizzle Tia Maria over the bottom layer.

To make ganache: Bring the cream and Tia Maria to the boil in a small saucepan. Take off the heat and add the dark chocolate bits, stir gently until the chocolate has melted.

To make topping: Prepare as for the ganache filling.

To assemble cake: Pour ganache filling over the bottom half of the cake, then place the other half of the cake on top. Refrigerate for half an hour. Remove the cake from the fridge and pour over the ganache topping. Allow to set at room temperature.

Strawberry and Blackcurrant Trifle

Serves 10

Blackcurrant Jelly
1 packet blackberry jelly crystals
350 ml (1⅓ cup) boiling water
100 ml (3 fl oz) Crème de Cassis
15 ml (½ fl oz) lemon juice
Pulp from 1 fresh lime

20-cm (8-in) sponge cake
2 punnets strawberries
60 ml (¼ cup) strawberry liqueur
500 ml (2 cups) vanilla custard
300 ml (1½ cups) thickened cream

To make jelly: Dissolve jelly crystals over boiling water then add Crème de Cassis, lemon juice and lime, mixing well. Pour into flat tray and set. Cut into cubes.

To assemble trifle: Cut the sponge into cubes. Soak the strawberries in the strawberry liqueur. In a large glass bowl layer the sponge, strawberries, jelly and custard. Decorate with whipped cream and strawberries.

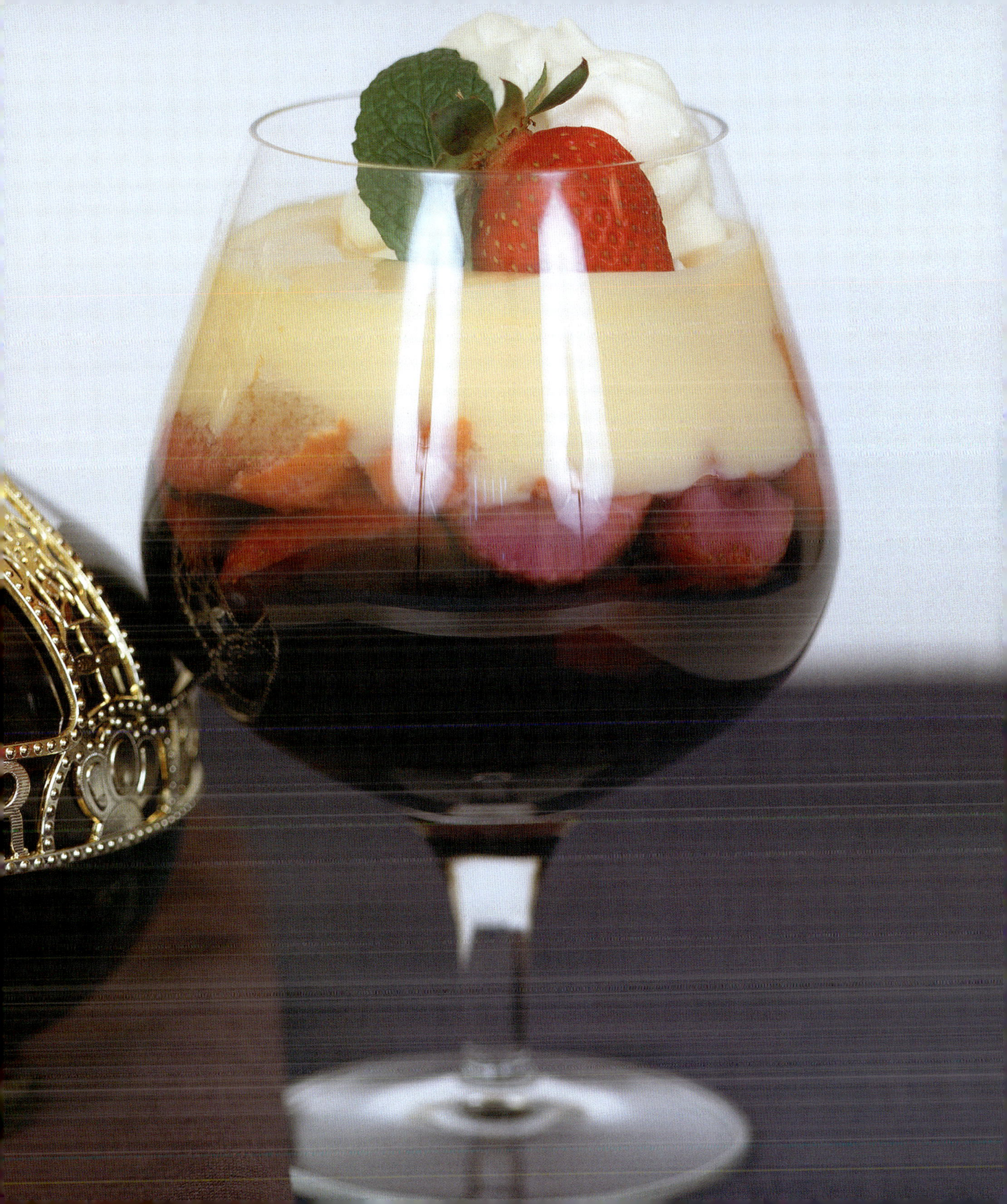

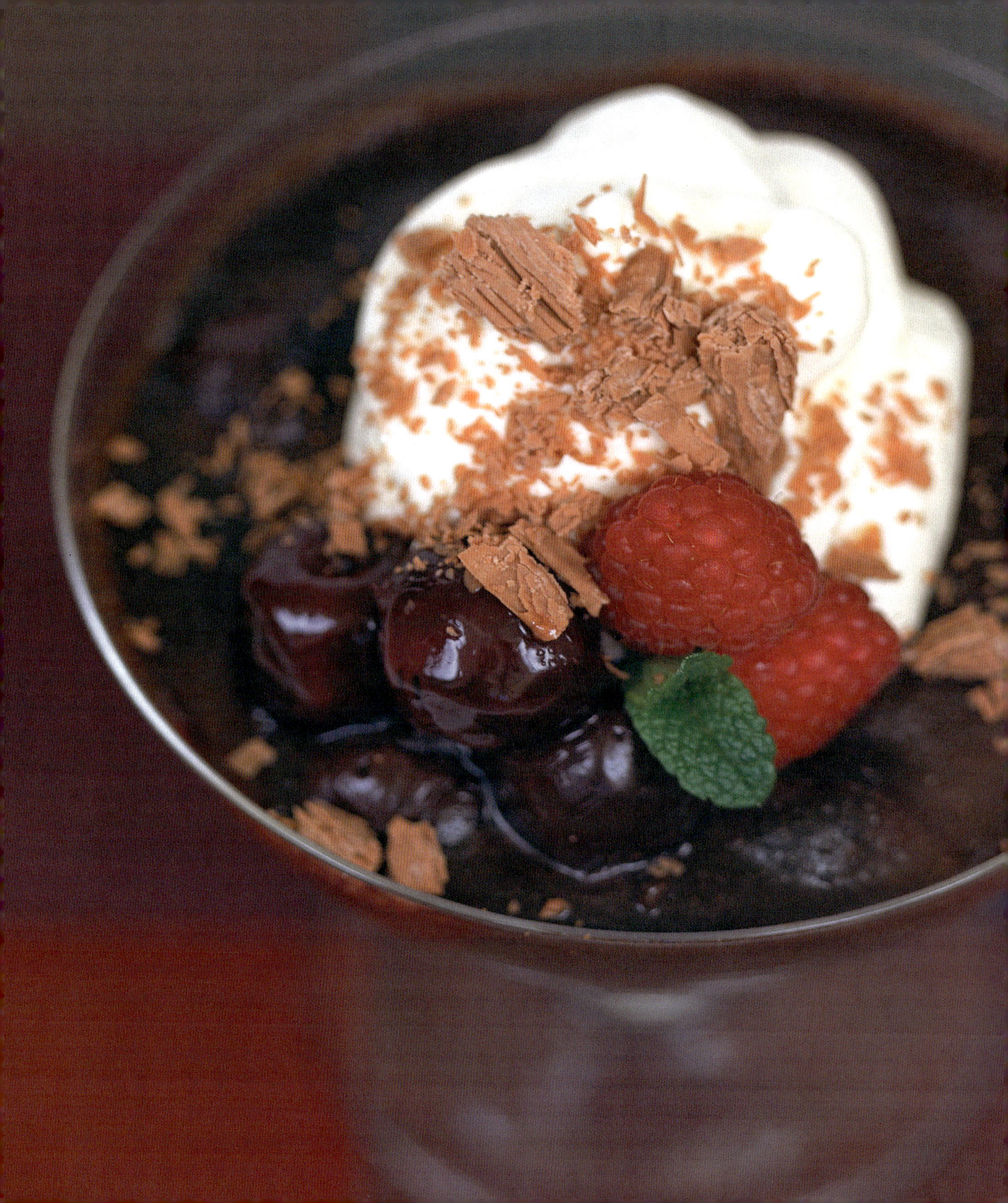

Cherry Ripe Trifle

Serves 10

Cherry Ripe Mousse
1 x 85 g (3 oz) packet chocolate instant pudding mix
250 ml (1 cup) cold milk
200 ml (7 fl oz) thickened cream
60 ml (¼ cup) Crème de Cacao
60 ml (¼ cup) cherry brandy
15 ml (½ fl oz) Malibu
1 tablespoon desiccated coconut

1 x 20-cm (8-inch) chocolate sponge cake
30 ml (1 fl oz) cherry brandy
300 ml (1½ cups) cream
1 x 425 g (12½ oz) can pitted cherries
125 ml (½ cup) desiccated coconut
2 x 30 g (1 oz) chocolate bars

To make the mousse: In a blender, blend the milk and cream with the instant pudding mix then add the alcohol and continue to blend. Add the coconut and process for a further second to mix in

To assemble trifle: Drizzle cherry brandy over chocolate sponge and cut cake into 2-cm (1-in) squares. Beat cream until thick. Place one-third of the chocolate cake chunks in the bottom of a glass bowl, top with one-third of the cherries and one-third of the desiccated coconut. Cover with one-third of the mousse mix then one-third of the cream. Keep layering until all ingredients are used; the last layer should be cream.

To garnish, break up the chocolate bars into small pieces and sprinkle over the top layer of cream.

Wildberry Whirl Parfait

Serves 6

1 punnet strawberries
1 x 85 g (3 oz) packet berry instant mousse mix
500 ml (2 cups) cold milk
60 ml (¼ cup) Chambord
60 ml (¼ cup) Cointreau
Whipped cream, extra strawberries and grated chocolate to garnish

Cut the strawberries in half, removing the stems. Place strawberries in a bowl and add the Cointreau then leave to marinate for approximately one hour in the refrigerator, tossing every so often.

Take the strawberries from the refrigerator. In a separate bowl, mix the instant mousse mix with hand beaters, blending in the Chambord and cold milk. Once mixed, layer the mousse then strawberries in parfait or large cocktail glasses and top with whipped cream, strawberries and grated chocolate.

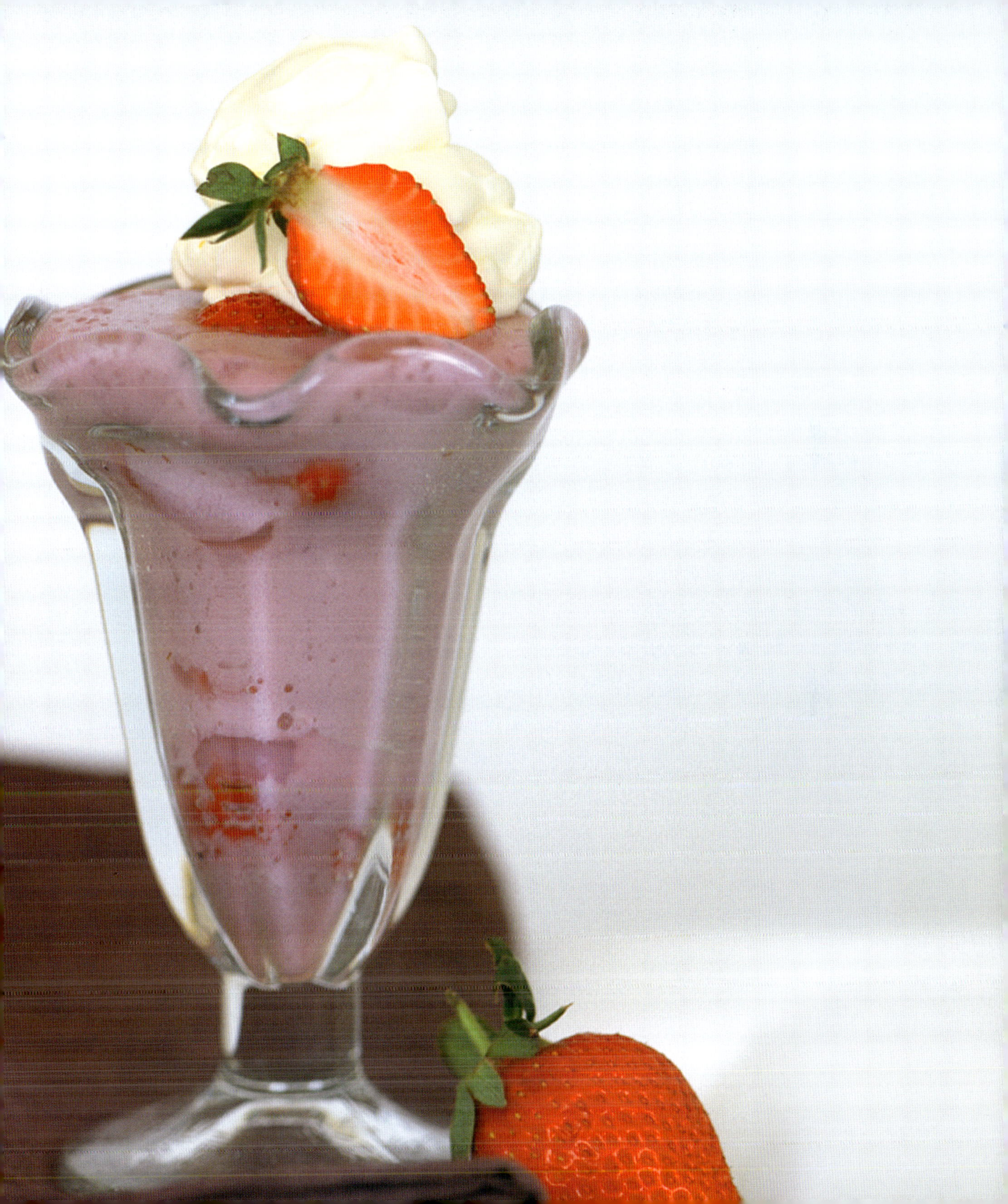

Crepes, fondues and dipping sauces

Crepes are delicious, thin pancakes perfect for
smothering with a heady, rich sauce.
Or try the fondues—old-fashioned but great fun; grab a
few friends and gather round…

Crepe Batter

Makes 15–18 crepes

2 eggs
2 tablespoons brandy
125 ml (½ cup) milk
Pinch salt
250 g (1 cup) plain flour
Butter for frying

Place eggs, brandy, milk, salt and flour in a food processor and process until smooth. Pour mixture into a jug, cover and stand for one hour. Check consistency and add more milk if necessary to make a thinner batter. Grease a 20-cm (8-inch) crepe pan with butter before making each crepe and stack in a pile, with a sheet of greaseproof paper separating each crepe.

Crepes with Toffee Sauce

Serves 8

Crepe Batter (see left)

Sauce
250 g (1 cup) brown sugar
250 ml (1 cup) double cream
100 g (3½ oz) butter
10 ml (⅓ oz) vanilla essence
60 ml (¼ cup) Grand Marnier

Make crepes as per recipe.

To make sauce: Mix brown sugar, cream, butter and vanilla essence in a saucepan. Heat until boiling and simmer for five minutes. Remove from heat and add the Grand Marnier.

Pour into a jug and serve poured over the crepes with your favourite ice-cream.

Crepes with Chocolate Sauce

Serves 8

Crepe Batter (see left)

Sauce
250 g (8 oz) dark chocolate
300 ml (1½ cups) thickened cream
3 tablespoons liqueur (such as Grand Marnier, Tia Maria, Kahlua or Cointreau)

Make crepes as per the recipe on opposite page.

To make sauce: Break chocolate into small pieces and melt on a very low heat, stirring continuously. Once melted, stir in cream then liqueur. Keep stirring over heat until the sauce has thickened.

Pour into a jug and serve poured over the crepes with your favourite ice-cream.

Crepes with Cointreau Cream Sauce

Serves 8

Crepe Batter (see page 88)

Make crepes as per the recipe on page 88.

Sauce
Grated rind and juice of one orange
125 ml (½ cup) castor sugar
¼ teaspoon ground ginger
Pinch of cinnamon
250 ml (1 cup) cream
90 ml (⅓ cup) Cointreau

Selection of seasonal fresh fruit, chopped

To make sauce: Blend all ingredients, except fruit, well, cover and chill for three hours. To serve, lay crepes on serving plates, top with fresh fruit then pour sauce over the top.

Lemon and Cointreau Sauce

Serves 8

Crepe Batter (see page 88)

Sauce
4 lemons, juiced
60 g (2 oz) castor sugar
45 ml (1½ fl oz) Cointreau
1 teaspoon cornflour

Make crepes as per the recipe on page 88.

To make sauce: Place lemon juice and sugar in a saucepan and heat until the sugar has dissolved, stir in Cointreau. In a separate dish, blend the cornflour with approximately 1 tablespoon of cold water and mix well. Gradually add to the saucepan stirring constantly; this will thicken the sauce.

Pour into a jug and serve poured over the crepes with double cream or your favourite ice-cream.

Fruit and Toffee Sauce Fondue

Serves 8

Selection of seasonal fresh fruit, chopped (such as pear slivers, banana slices, strawberries and mandarin wedges)

Sauce
250 g (1 cup) brown sugar
250 ml (1 cup) double cream
10 ml (⅓ oz) vanilla essence
100 g (3½ oz) butter
60 ml (¼ cup) Grand Marnier

Arrange fruit attractively on a serving plate.

To make sauce: Mix brown sugar, cream, vanilla essence and butter in a saucepan. Heat until boiling and simmer for five minutes. Remove from heat and add the Grand Marnier. Pour the sauce into a dipping bowl and let guests help themselves.

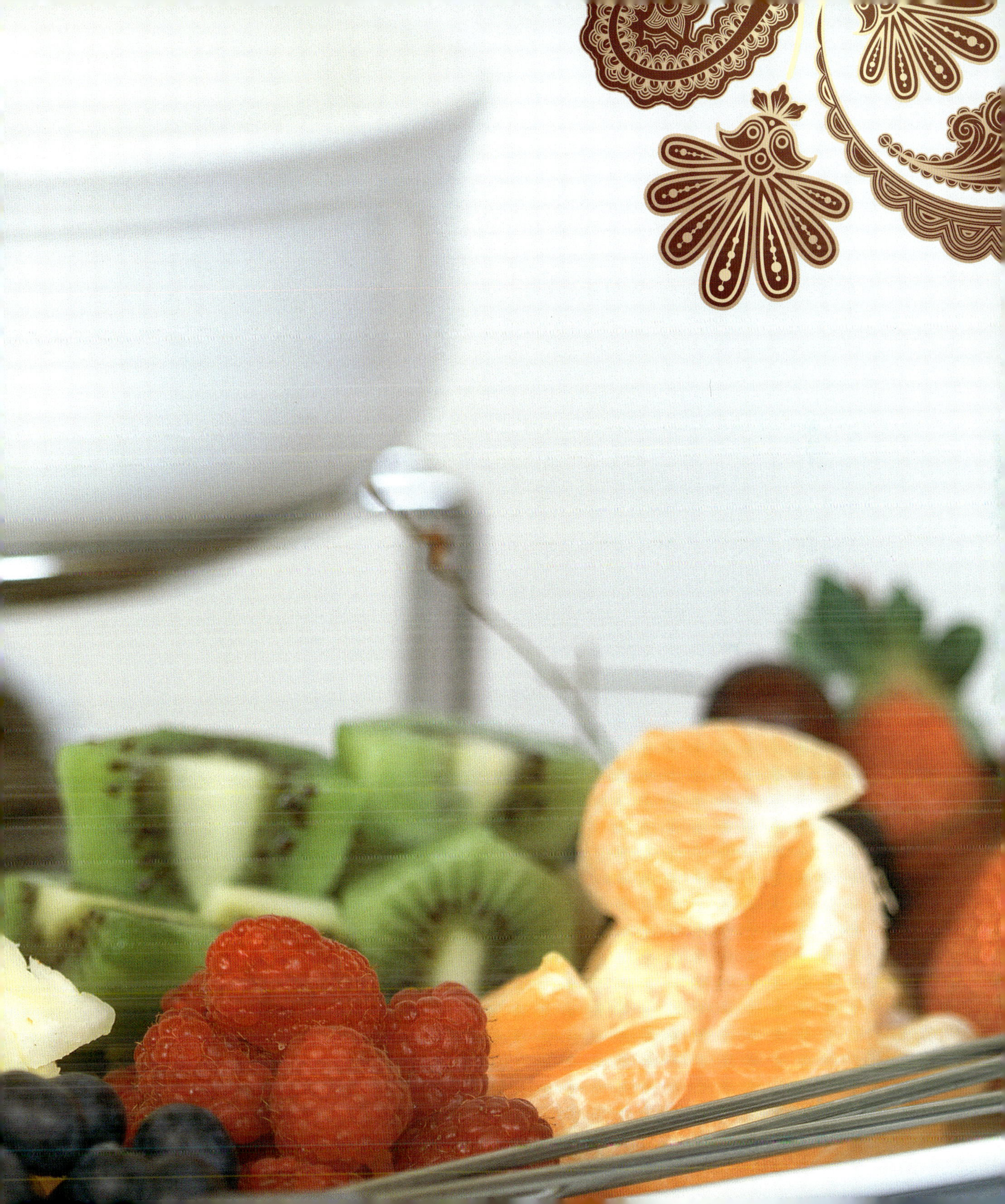

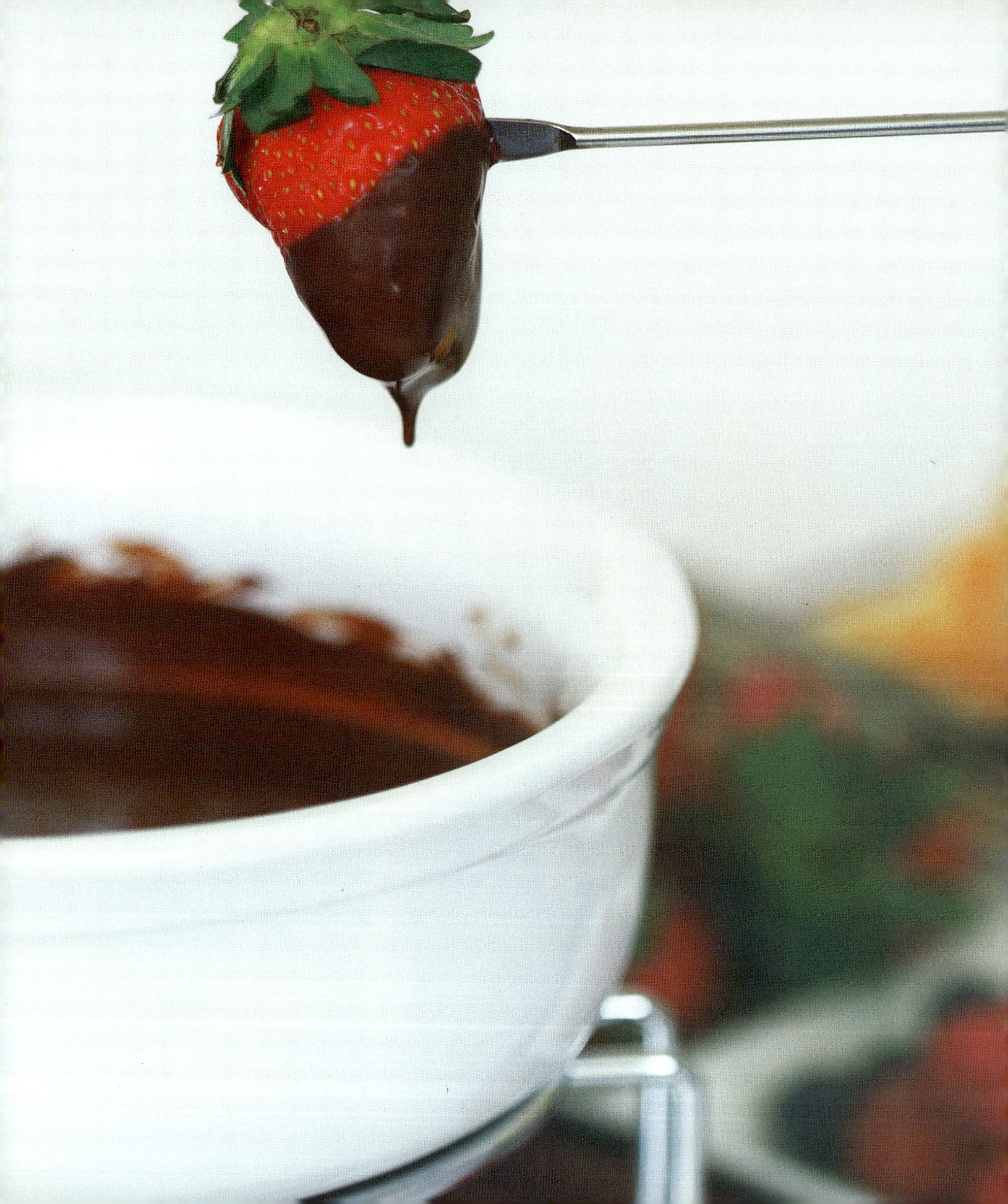

Chocolate and Fruit Fondue

Serves 8

Sauce
250 g (8 oz) dark chocolate
300 ml (1½ cups) thickened cream
3 tablespoons liqueur (such as Grand Marnier, Tia Maria, Kahlua or Cointreau)

Selection of seasonal fresh fruit, chopped (such as pear slivers, banana slices, strawberries and mandarin wedges)

Break chocolate into small pieces and melt on a very low heat, stirring continuously. Once melted, stir in cream then liqueur. Keep stirring over heat until the sauce has thickened. Place sauce in a fondue bowl over a flame.

Arrange desired fruits on a platter and serve with fondue forks.

Fruit Platter with Cointreau Cream Sauce

Serves 8

Sauce
Grated rind and juice of 1 orange
125 ml (½ cup) castor sugar
¼ teaspoon ground ginger
Pinch of cinnamon
250 ml (1 cup) cream
90 ml (⅓ cup) Cointreau

Large platter of seasonal fresh fruit, chopped

To make sauce: Blend all ingredients well, cover and chill for three hours.

Arrange fruit attractively on a serving plate. Place sauce in bowl in centre of platter. Provide toothpicks for guests to pick up fruit and dip in sauce.

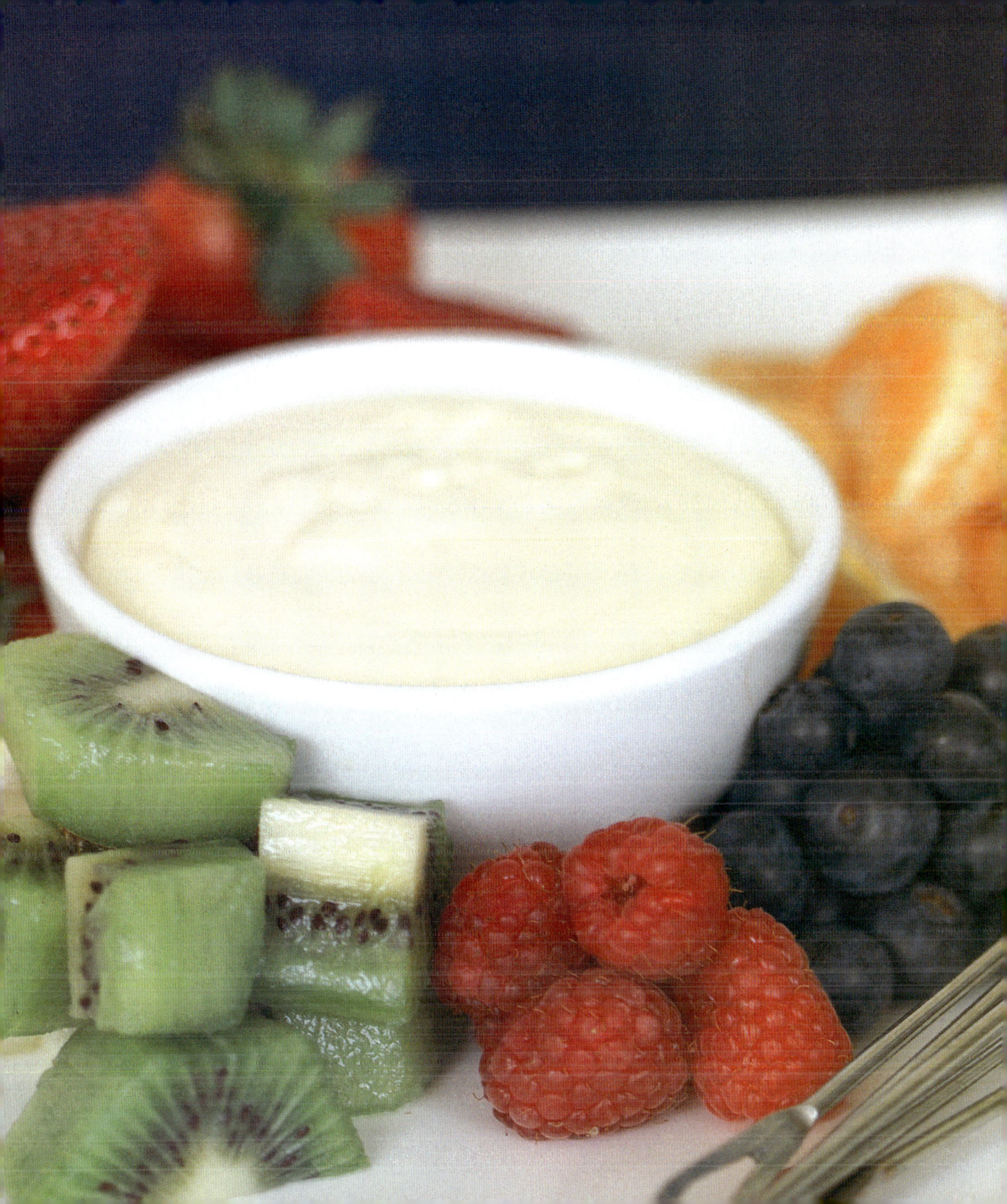

Marinated fruits

These spiced-up fruit recipes make a sensational end to a meal—beautiful to look at and very tempting to the tastebuds. Cool, refreshing finales for hot summer nights.

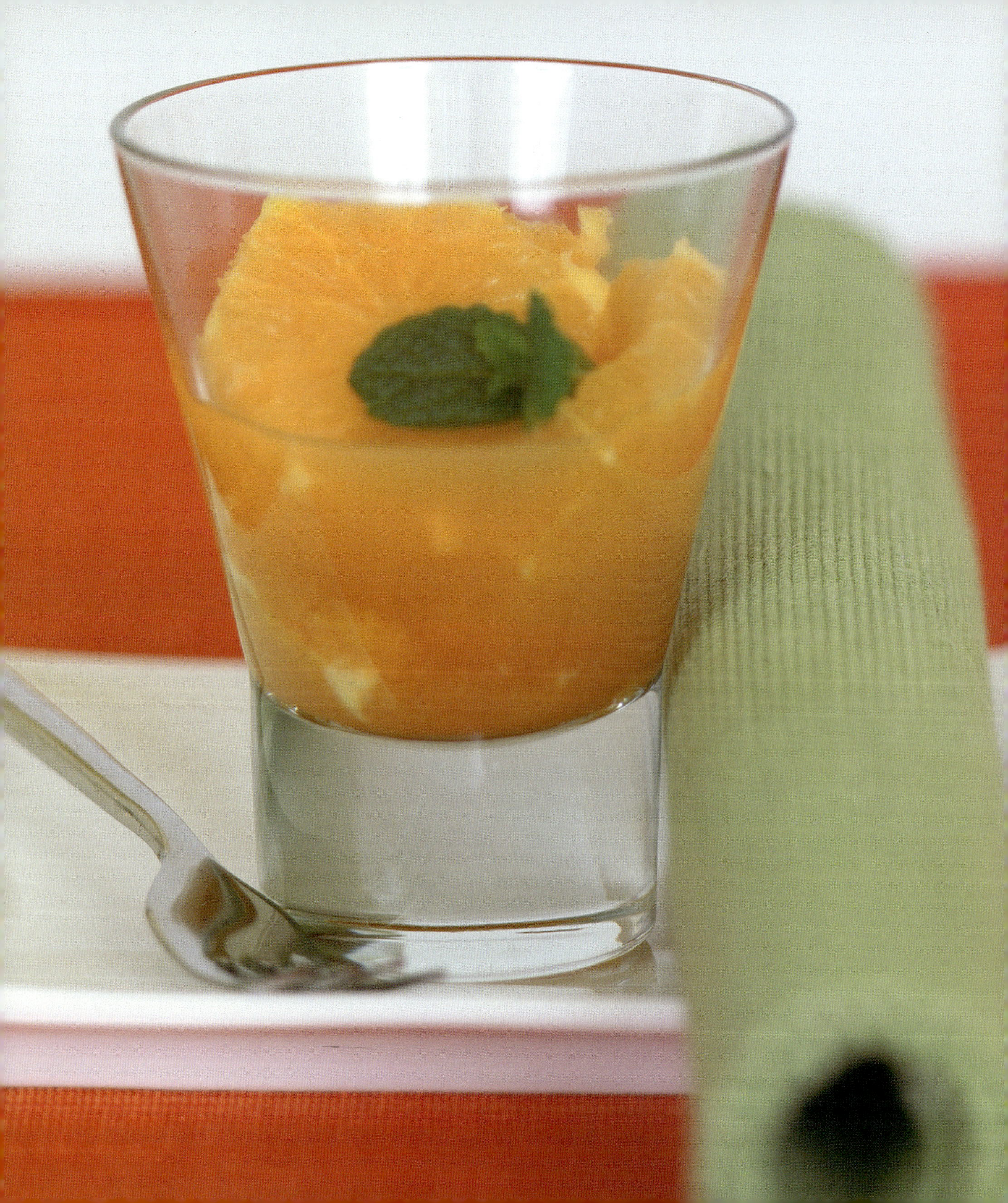

Spiced Orange Slices

Serves 8

8 medium to large oranges
125 ml (½ cup) castor sugar
1 teaspoon ground ginger
½ teaspoon cinnamon
60 g (2 oz) teaspoon nutmeg
150 ml (2/3 cup) Grand Marnier

Peel oranges, removing all pith. Slice oranges thinly on a plate to retain juices. Mix sugar with the spices, then add orange juice and Grand Marnier.

In a glass bowl, layer orange slices then pour over juices. Place in the refrigerator to chill before serving.

Watermelon Boat

Serves 16

1 watermelon (with reserved juice)
2 oranges
1 punnet strawberries
1 apple
90 ml (⅓ cup) vodka
60 ml (¼ cup) Cointreau
60 ml (¼ cup) strawberry liqueur

Place watermelon on a table to locate balancing point. Cut one-third off the top of the watermelon so that it sits level. Hollow out watermelon, removing seeds and retaining juice. (Hollowing out the watermelon over a large bowl or saucepan makes it easier to retain juices.)

Use the large portion of the watermelon as a bowl. Cut watermelon flesh and other fruit into medium-sized chunks, reserving juices. Mix fruit and place into the watermelon shell. Mix the alcohol with any fruit juices saved and pour over the arranged fruit. Place in the refrigerator to chill and marinate.

To serve, place on table as is and provide toothpicks for guests to pick up the fruit.

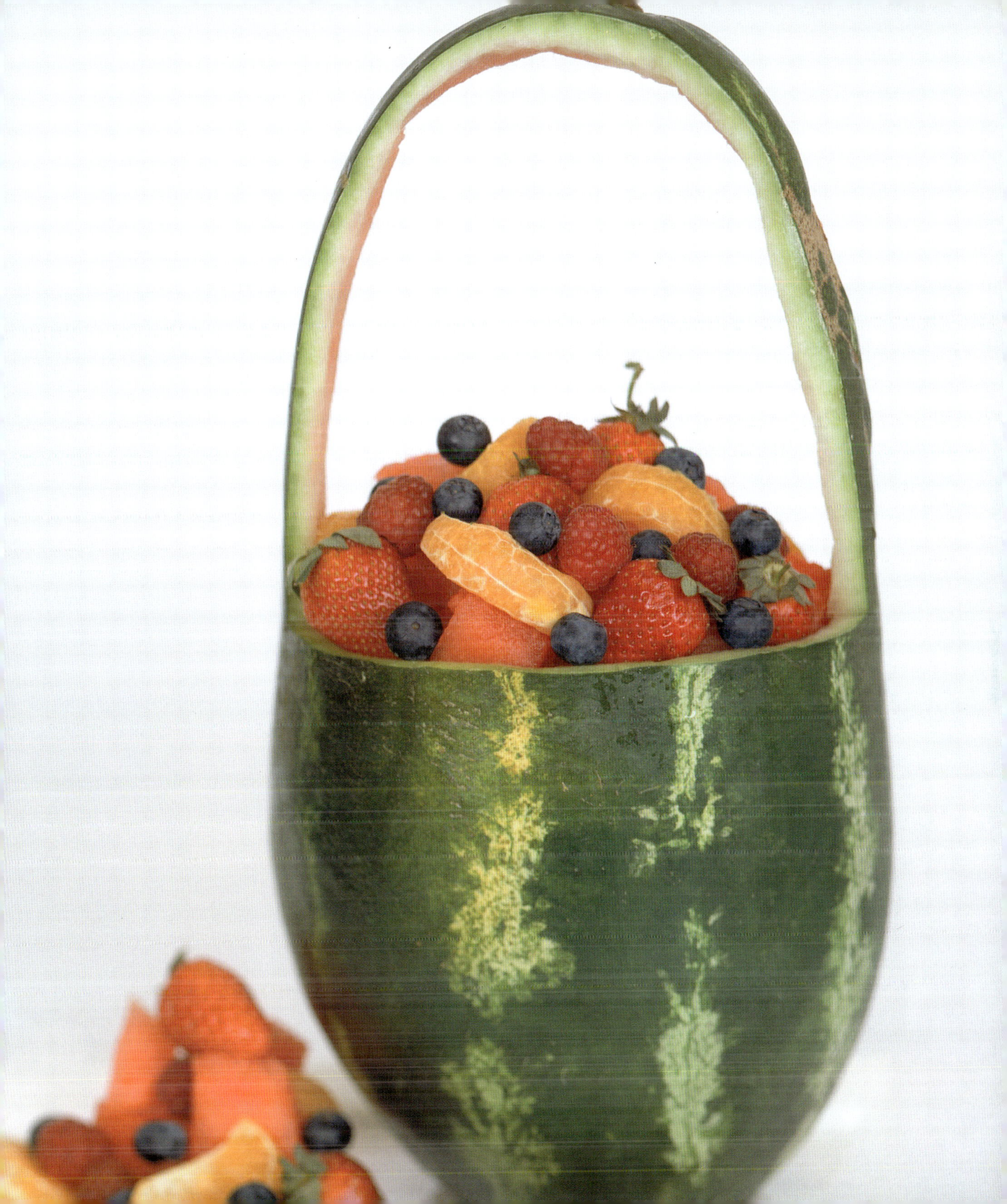

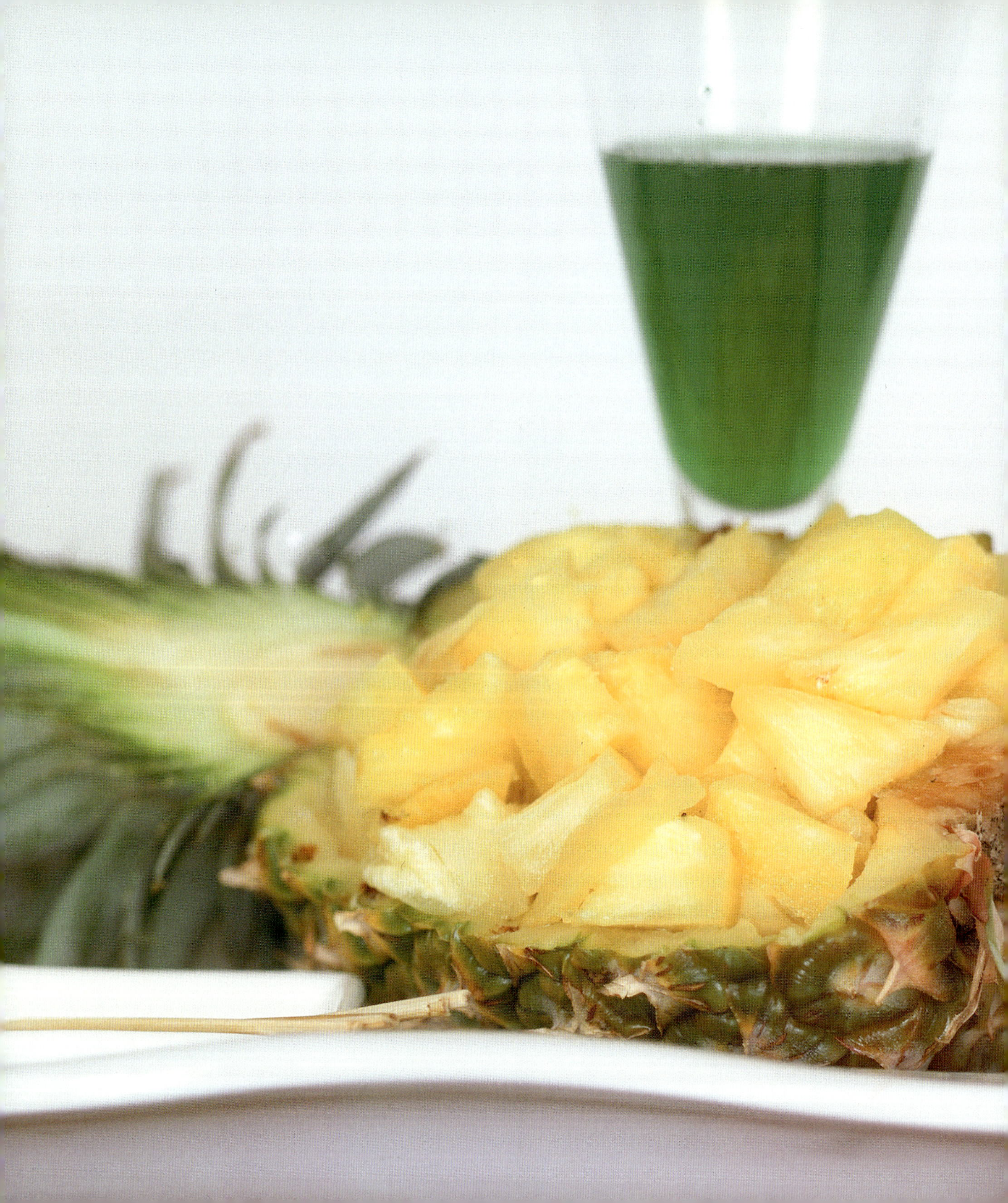

Liquid Ecstasy Pineapple Boat

Serves 10-12

1 pineapple
60 ml (¼ cup) pineapple juice (with reserved juice)
90 ml (⅓ cup) Midori
45 ml (1½ fl oz) Bacardi
15 ml (½ oz) Malibu
45 ml (1½ fl oz) Blue Curacao
60 ml (¼ cup) lemon juice

Cut the pineapple in half from head to base, keeping the head attached. Hollow out the pineapple, and cut pineapple flesh into pieces, retaining the juice. Place cubed pineapple back into the two pineapple shells. Mix the pineapple juice with the alcohol and pour over pineapple pieces. Place in the refrigerator to chill.

To serve, place on table as is and provide toothpicks for guests to pick up the fruit.

Honeydew Melon Delight

Serves 8-10

1 honeydew melon
90 ml (⅓ cup) lemon juice
90 ml (⅓ cup) Midori
90 ml (⅓ cup) Cointreau

Cut honeydew melon in half and remove seeds. Remove melon flesh from shell keeping shell intact. Cut melon flesh into chunks and return to shell halves. Mix lemon juice and alcohol and pour over melon. Place in the refrigerator to chill.

To serve, place on table as is and provide toothpicks for guests to pick up the fruit.

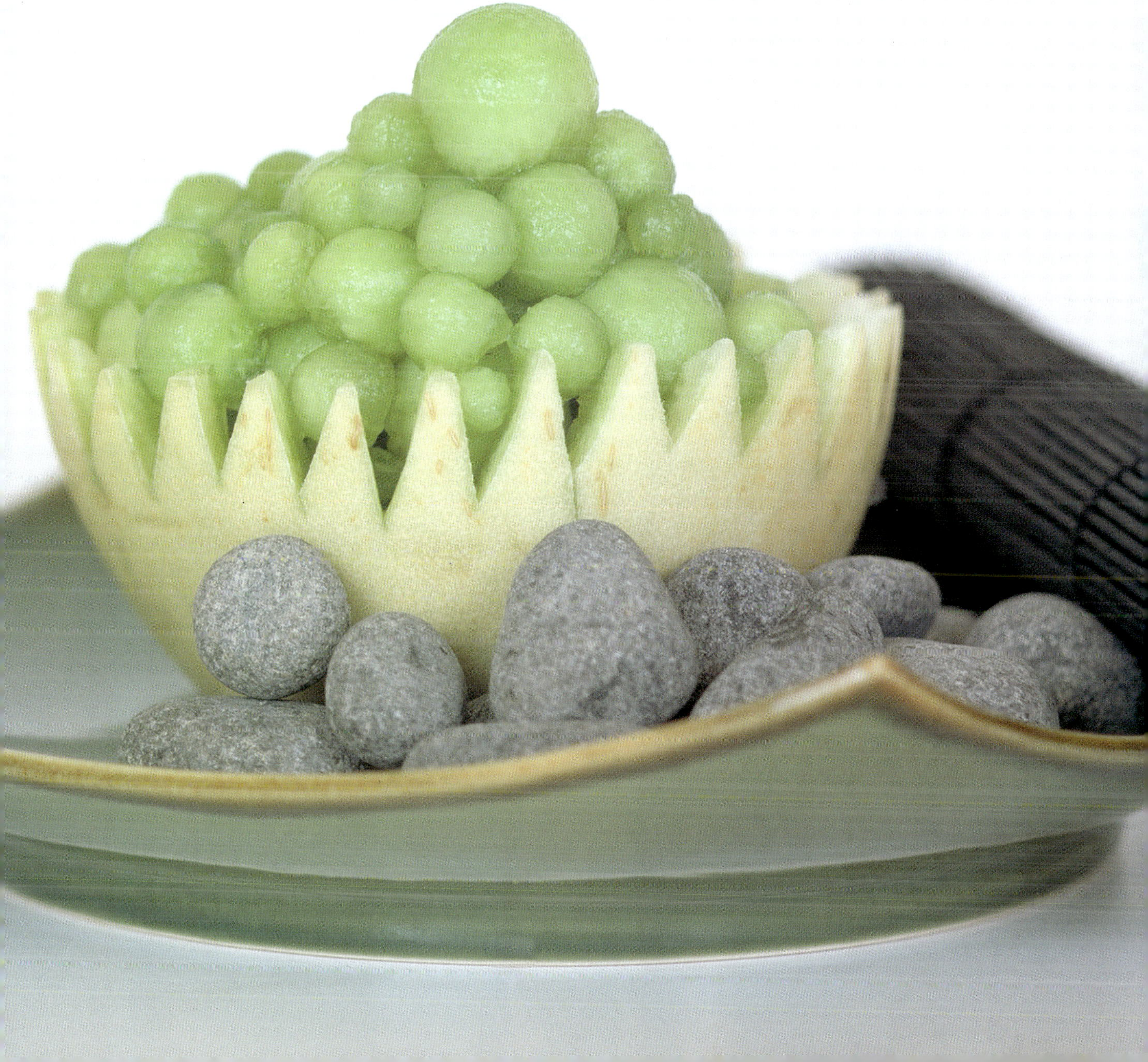

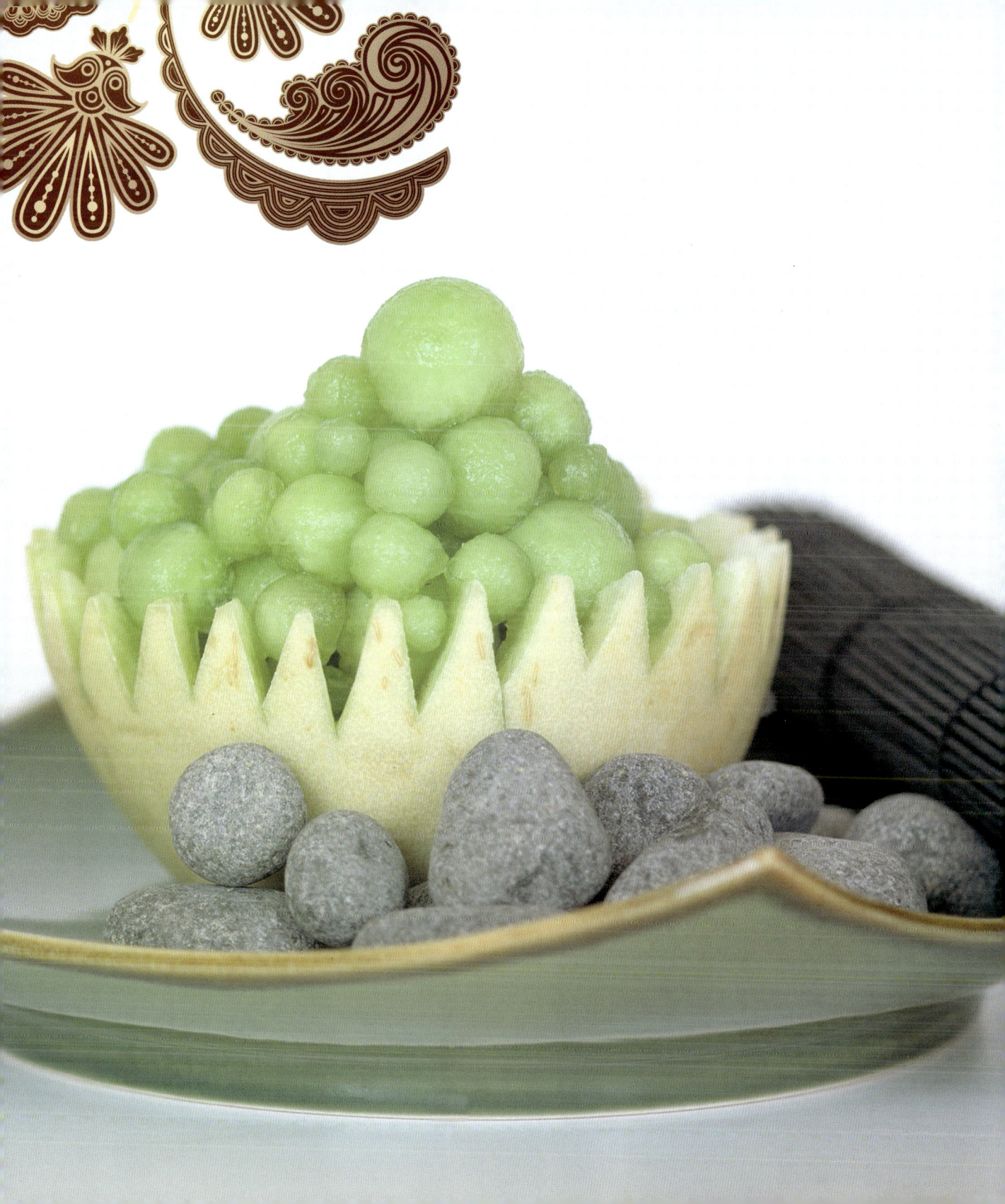

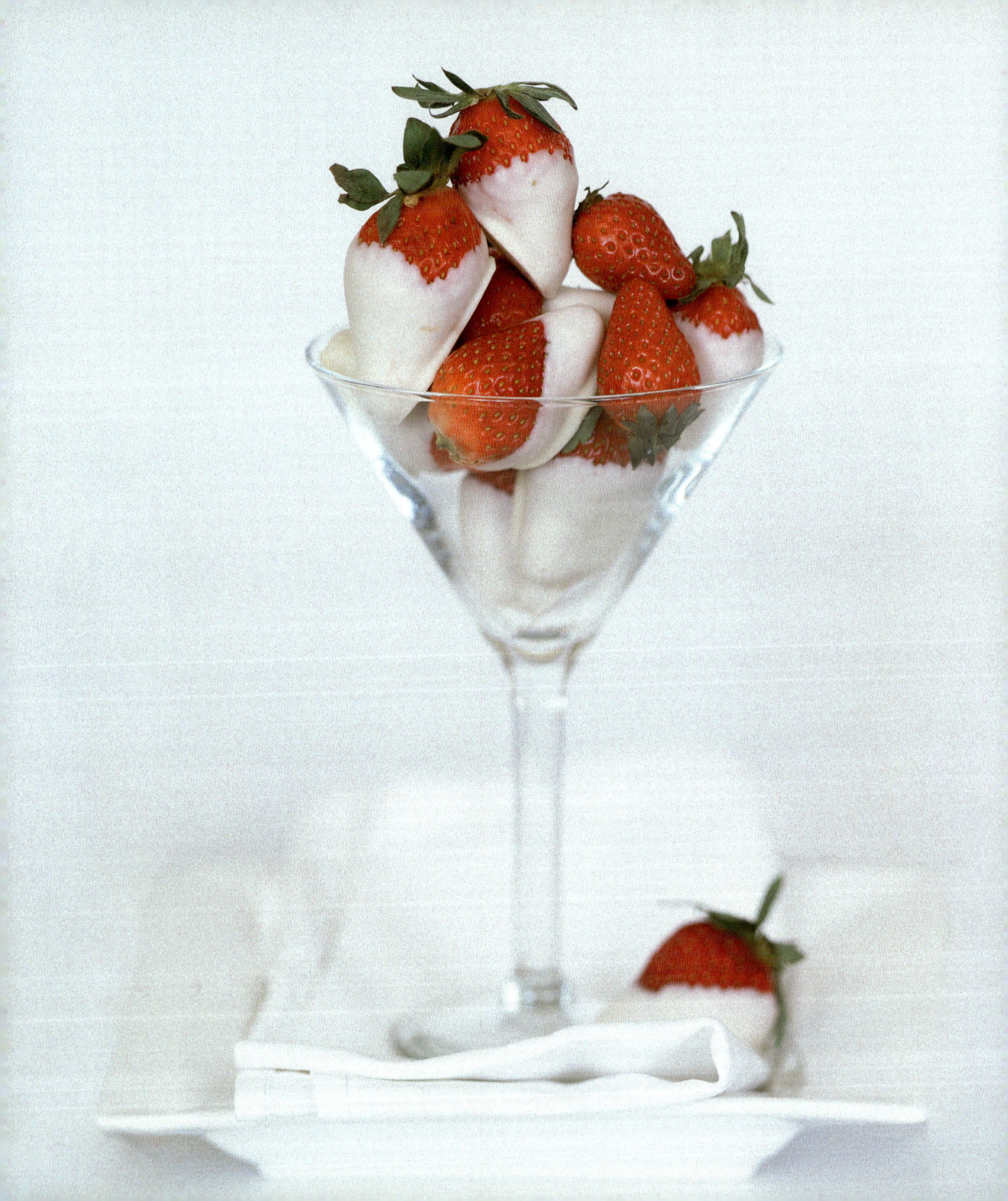

Cointreau-infused Strawberries

200 g (7 oz) block of white cooking chocolate
2 punnets large strawberries
Cointreau

Melt cooking chocolate in a double saucepan. Wash strawberries then leave to drain. Fill a medical syringe (purchase at your local pharmacy) with Cointreau, insert syringe into the middle of each strawberry and fill using the pressure to gauge whether the strawberry is full or not. Once full roll the base of each strawberry in the melted chocolate and place on a tray. Place the tray in the refrigerator for the chocolate to set.

Baileys-infused Strawberries

200 g (7 oz) block milk cooking chocolate
2 punnets large strawberries
Baileys Irish Cream

Melt cooking chocolate in a double saucepan. Wash strawberries then leave to drain. Fill a medical syringe (purchase at your local pharmacy) with Baileys Irish Cream, insert syringe into the middle of each strawberry and fill using the pressure to gauge whether the strawberry is full or not. Once full roll the base of each strawberry in the melted chocolate and place on a tray. Place the tray in the refrigerator for the chocolate to set.

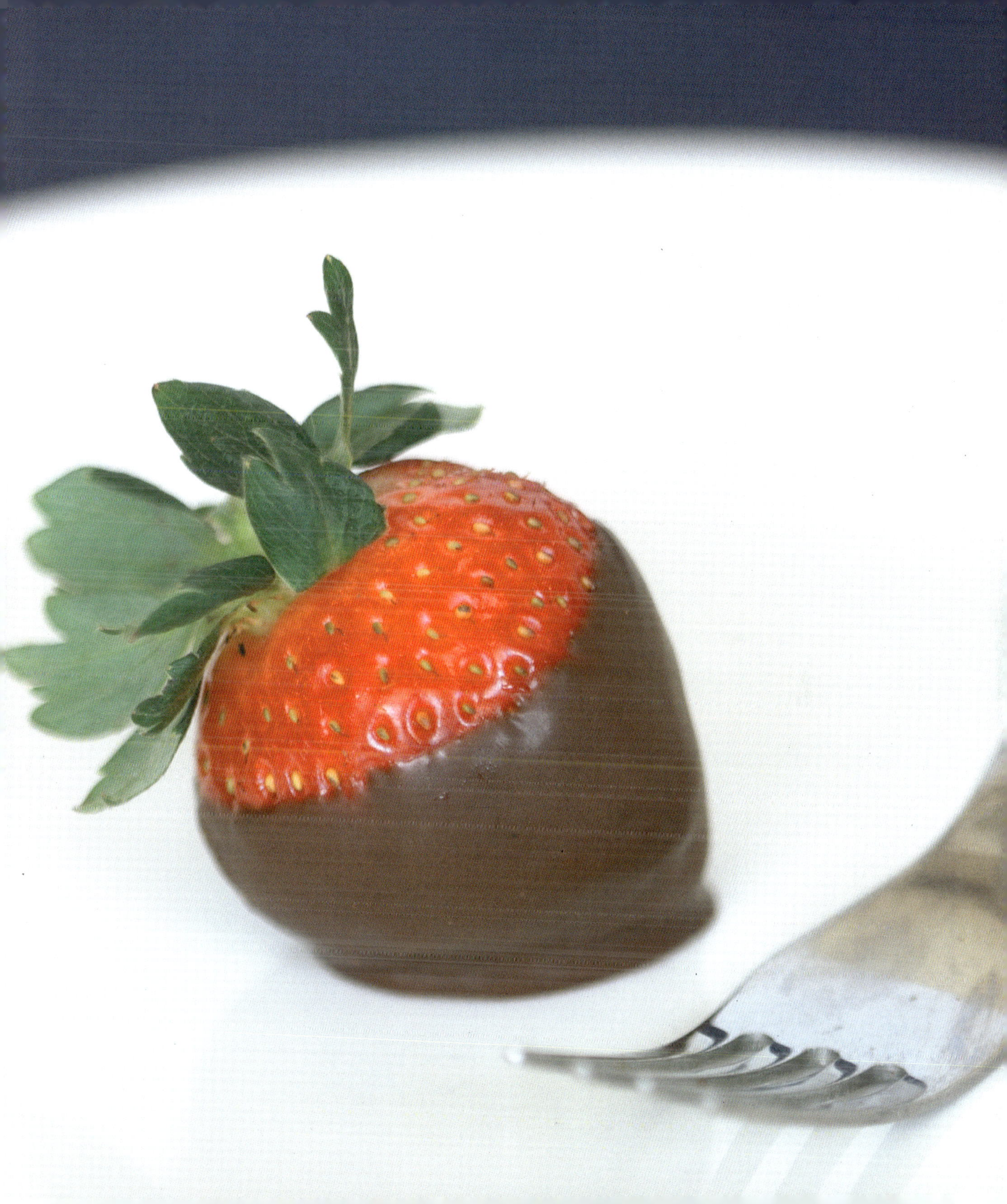

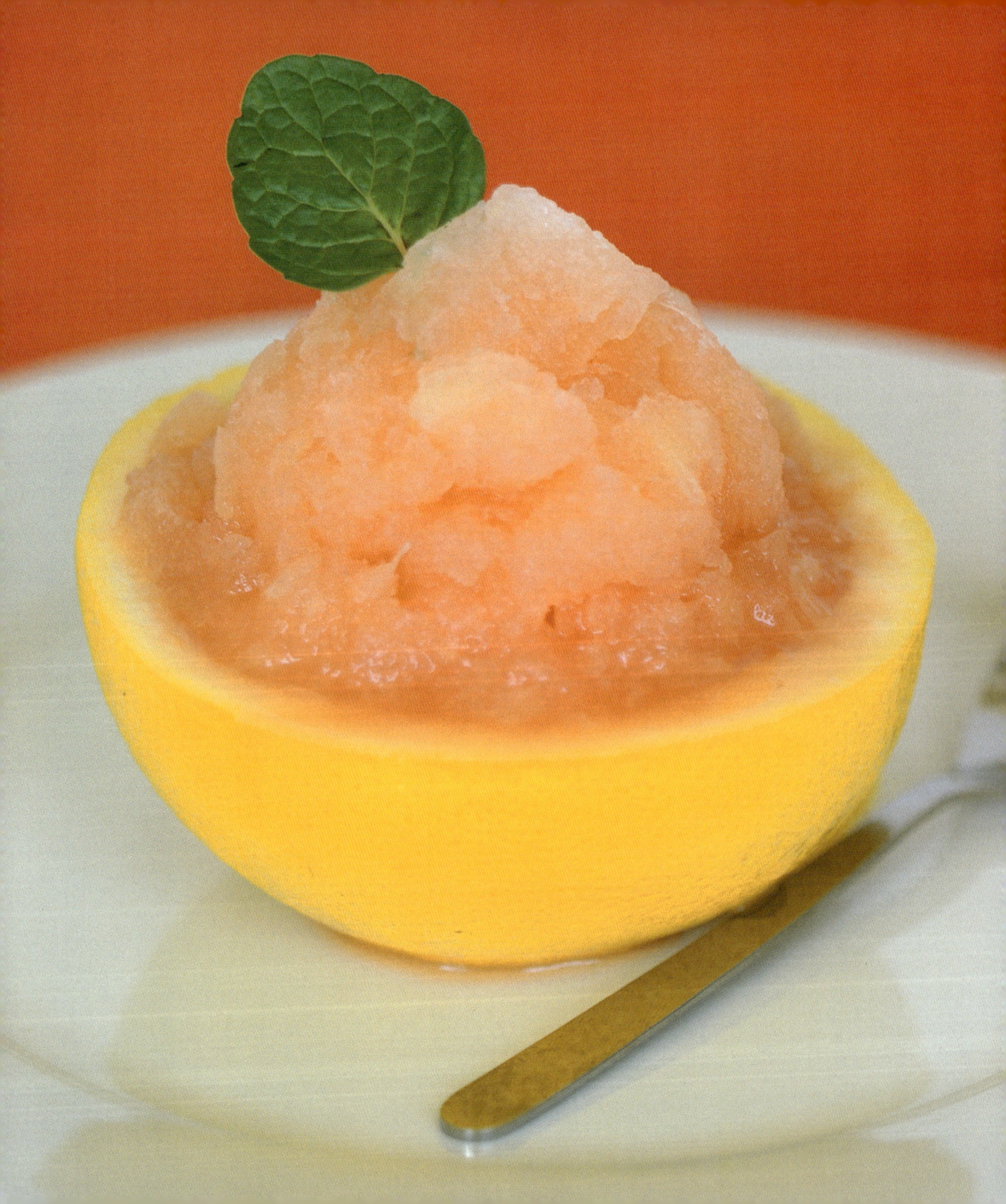

Grapefruit and Campari Sorbet

Serves 8

4 grapefruits
60 ml (¼ cup) gin
90 ml (⅓ cup) Campari
250 ml (1 cup) cranberry juice
2 tablespoons castor sugar
8 ice cubes

Cut the grapefruits in half and hollow out, place the pulp in a blender. Add alcohol, cranberry juice and sugar to the blender and blend. Add ice cubes and blend well. Pour mixture into the grapefruit shells and freeze overnight.

Dessert shots

These quick and easy desserts can be whipped up and refrigerated up to two days before a party. Plastic, disposable shot glasses are a handy way to serve the dessert shots. Delightful! Hand your guests a spoon and tell them to go for it.

Butterscotch and Chocolate Mousse Shots

Serves 20

1 x 85 g (3 oz) packet chocolate instant pudding mix
200 ml (7 fl oz) cold milk
250 ml (1 cup) cold thickened cream
75 ml (2½ oz) Baileys Irish Cream
75 ml (2½ oz) butterscotch liqueur or butterscotch schnapps
1 x 30 g (1 oz) flakey chocolate bar to garnish

Make pudding using the milk and cream as per instructions, adding the alcohol at the end. Pour mixture into shot glasses and garnish with crumbled chocolate bar pieces. Refrigerate to set.

Scottish Mousse Shots

Serves 15

200 ml (7 fl oz) cream
150 ml (2/3 cup) milk
1 egg, beaten
60 ml (¼ cup) Scotch whisky
45 ml (1½ fl oz) Drambuie
1 sachet of gelatin

In a saucepan, stir together cream, milk, egg and alcohol and bring to a simmer. Sprinkle gelatin over mix and stir in until it dissolves. Whisk until aerated. Pour into shot glasses and refrigerate to set. Garnish with whipped cream and chocolate powder if desired.

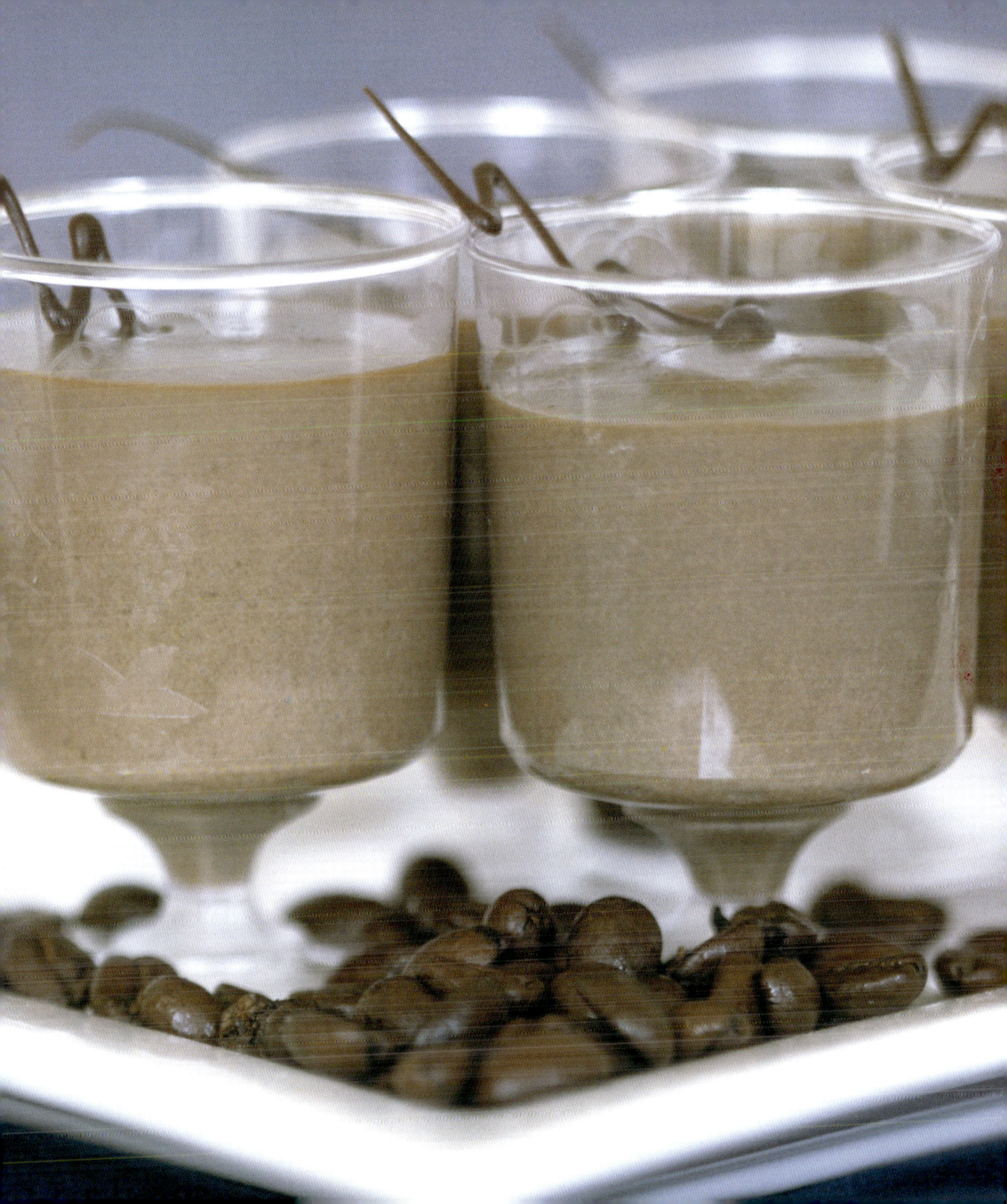

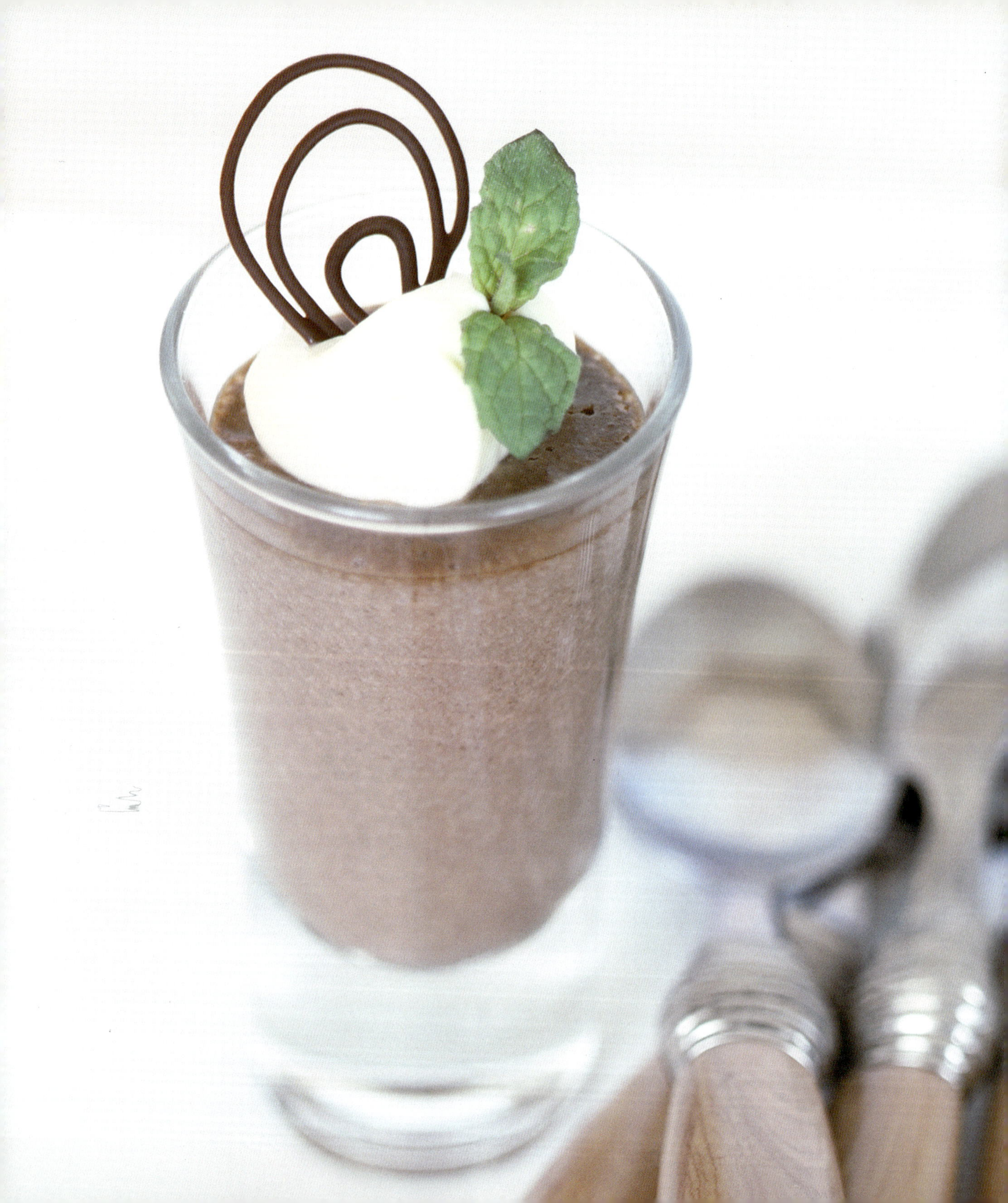

Choc Mint Mousse Shots

Serves 20

1 x 85 g (3 oz) packet chocolate instant pudding mix
200 ml (7 fl oz) milk
200 ml (7 fl oz) thickened cream
75 ml (2½ fl oz) Crème De Menthe
125 ml (½ cup) Baileys Irish Cream
1 x 30 g (1 oz) flakey chocolate bar to garnish

Make pudding using the milk and cream as per instructions, adding the alcohol at the end. Pour into shot glasses and garnish with chocolate bar pieces. Refrigerate to set.

Cherry Ripe Mousse Shots

Serves 20

1 x 85 g (3 oz) packet chocolate instant pudding mix
180 ml (¾ cup) cold milk
200 ml (7 fl oz) thickened cream
100 ml (3½ fl oz) Crème de Cacao
100 ml (3½ fl oz) cherry brandy
1 tablespoon desiccated coconut
30 ml (1 fl oz) Malibu
1 x 30 g (1 oz) flakey chocolate bar

Make pudding using the milk and cream as per instructions, adding the coconut and alcohol at the end. Pour into disposable shot glasses and garnish with crumbled chocolate bar. Refrigerate to set.

Mocha Custard Delights

Serves 10

180 g (6 oz) sugar
4 egg yolks
2 eggs
60 ml (¼ cup) Kahlua
30 ml (1 fl oz) Baileys Irish Cream
400 ml (1¾ cups) milk
250 ml (1 cup) cream
60 g (2 oz) dark chocolate
1 tablespoon coffee powder

Preheat the oven to 170°C (340°F). Beat the sugar, egg yolks, eggs, Kahlua and Baileys together until smooth. Heat the milk, cream, chocolate and coffee powder together in a saucepan until the chocolate melts and the mixture is almost simmering. Stir well. While whisking, pour the hot milk into the egg mixture, stirring all the time until the custard is well combined. Pour into a jug with a spout and divide evenly between ten small soufflé dishes or coffee cups.

Place the dishes or cups in a baking dish and pour in hot water to come halfway up the sides. Bake in preheated oven for 40 minutes or until the custard is just set. Cool then chill until ready to serve. To serve, decorate with whipped cream, chocolate and coffee sprinkles.

Vanilla and Frangelico Mousse Shots

Serves 20

1 x 85g (3 oz) packet vanilla instant pudding mix
300 ml (1½ cups) milk
200 ml (7 fl oz) cream
100 ml (3½ fl oz) Frangelico
1 cup crushed almonds
Almonds, whipped cream and cinnamon to garnish

Make pudding using the milk and cream as per instructions, adding the liqueur and crushed almonds at the end. Pour into shot glasses and garnish with almond pieces, cream and cinnamon. Refrigerate to set.

Vanilla and Frangelico
Mousse Shots

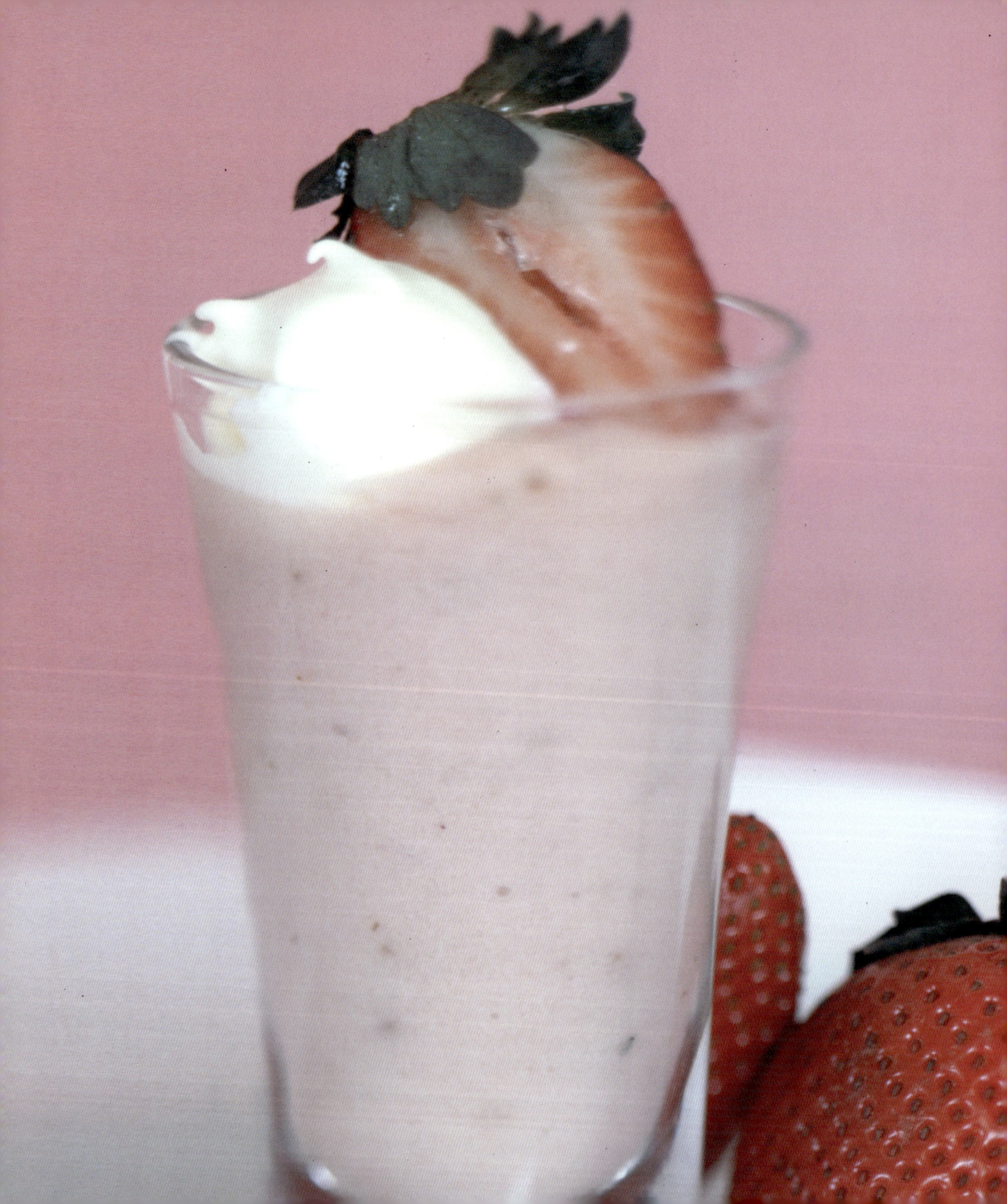

Vanilla and Strawberry Mousse Shots

Serves 20

1 x 85 g (3 oz) packet vanilla instant pudding mix
300 ml (1½ cups) milk
200 ml (7 fl oz) cream
100 ml (3½ fl oz) strawberry liqueur
1 punnet strawberries
Extra strawberries and whipped cream to garnish

Make pudding using the milk and cream as per instructions, adding the liqueur and strawberries at the end. Pour into shot glasses and garnish with strawberries and cream. Refrigerate to set.

Vanilla, Peach and Mango Mousse Shots

Serves 20

1 x 85 g (3 oz) packet vanilla instant pudding mix
300 ml (1½ cups) milk
200 ml (7 fl oz) cream
100 ml (3½ fl oz) mango liqueur
1 x 200 g (6½ oz) can peaches, cut into small pieces, discard juice
Extra peach pieces, whipped cream and cinnamon to garnish

Make pudding using the milk and cream as per instructions, adding the liqueur and peaches at the end. Pour into shot glasses and garnish with extra peach pieces, cream and cinnamon. Refrigerate to set.

Vanilla and Blackberry Mousse Shots

Serves 20

1 x 85 g (3 oz) packet vanilla instant pudding mix
300 ml (1½ cups) milk
200 ml (7 fl oz) cream
100 ml (3½ fl oz) Chambord
1 punnet blackberries, cut in half
Extra blackberries and whipped cream to garnish

Make pudding using the milk and cream as per instructions, adding the liqueur and blackberry pieces at the end. Pour into shot glasses and garnish with blackberries and cream. Refrigerate to set.

Vanilla and Banana Mousse Shots

Serves 20

1 x 85 g (3 oz) packet vanilla instant pudding mix
300 ml (1½ cups) milk
200 ml (7 fl oz) cream
100 ml (3½ fl oz) banana liqueur
2 bananas, pureed
Whipped cream and nutmeg to garnish

Make pudding using the milk and cream as per instructions, adding the liqueur and bananas at the end. Pour into shot glasses and garnish with cream and nutmeg. Refrigerate to set.

Vanilla, Honey and Cinnamon Mousse Shots

Serves 20

1 x 85 g (3 oz) packet vanilla instant pudding mix
300 ml (1½ cups) milk
200 ml (7 fl oz) cream
100 ml (3½ fl oz) Medos Honey Vodka
25 ml honey
½ teaspoon cinnamon
Whipped cream and extra cinnamon to garnish

Make pudding using the milk and cream as per instructions, adding the vodka and honey at the end. Pour into shot glasses and garnish with cream and cinnamon. Refrigerate to set.

Jelly shots

This is not jelly as you remember it! This is special—fruity, alcoholic jelly served in shot glasses for a fun end to a meal.

Cosmopolitan Jelly Shots

Serves 20

1 packet raspberry jelly crystals
200 ml (7 fl oz) boiling water
150 ml (2/3 cup) cranberry juice
2 limes, freshly squeezed with pulp
75 ml (2½ fl oz) vodka
75 ml (2½ fl oz) Cointreau

Dissolve jelly crystals over boiling water. Stir in cranberry juice, lime, vodka and Cointreau. Pour into shot glasses and refrigerate to set, preferably overnight.

Blackcurrant Jelly Shots

Serves 20

1 packet blackberry jelly crystals
300 ml (1½ cups) boiling water
150 ml (5 fl oz) Crème de Cassis
15 ml (½ fl oz) lemon juice
Pulp from 1 fresh lime
Pulp from 2 passionfruit

Dissolve jelly crystals over boiling water. Stir in Crème de Cassis, lemon juice, lime and passionfruit, mixing well. Pour into shot glasses and refrigerate to set, preferably overnight.

Cosmopolitan
Jelly Shots

Galliano and Champagne Jelly Shots

Serves 20

1 packet orange jelly crystals
200 ml (7 fl oz) of boiling water
60 ml (¼ cup) Galliano
250 ml (1 cup) sweet champagne

Dissolve jelly crystals over boiling water, leave to cool. Add Galliano, stirring well, then top with champagne. Pour into shot glasses and refrigerate to set, preferably overnight.

Fresh Peach Jelly Shots

Serves 20

1 packet orange jelly crystals
90 ml (⅓ cup) peach liqueur
60 ml (¼ cup) orange liqueur
250 ml (1 cup) boiling water
60 ml (¼ cup) peach nectar
3 limes squeezed
4 large peaches, stones removed and cut into small pieces

Dissolve jelly crystals in boiling water. Stir in alcohol, nectar and juice, mixing well. Add peach pieces, stir and pour into shot glasses. Refrigerate to set, preferably overnight.

Galliano and
Champagne Jelly Shots

Campari Jelly Shots

Serves 20

1 packet orange jelly crystals
90 ml (⅓ cup) Campari
60 ml (¼ cup) gin
100 ml (3½ fl oz) grapefruit juice
250 ml (1 cup) boiling water

Dissolve jelly crystals in boiling water. Stir in alcohol and juice, mixing well. Pour into shot glasses then refrigerate to set, preferably overnight.

Midori Splice Jelly Shots

Serves 20

1 packet pineapple jelly crystals
250 ml (1 cup) boiling water
125 ml (½ cup) Midori
30 ml (1 fl oz) Cointreau
30 ml (1 fl oz) Malibu
60 ml (¼ cup) cream

Dissolve jelly crystals in boiling water. Stir in alcohol and then cream, mixing well. Pour into shot glasses and refrigerate to set, preferably overnight.

Chi Chi Jelly Shots

Serves 20

1 packet pineapple jelly crystals
250 ml (1 cup) boiling water
90 ml (⅓ cup) vodka
60 ml (¼ cup) Malibu
90 ml (⅓ cup) coconut cream

Dissolve jelly crystals in boiling water, leave to cool. Stir in alcohol and coconut cream, mixing well. Pour into shot glasses and refrigerate to set, preferably overnight.

Berry Royale Jelly Shots

Serves 20

1 packet raspberry jelly crystals
200 ml (7 fl oz) boiling water
100 ml (3½ fl oz) Chambord
200 ml (7 fl oz) champagne

Dissolve jelly crystals over boiling water then stir in Chambord. Half fill shot glasses then top with champagne. Refrigerate to set, preferably overnight.

Orange, Ginger and Passionfruit Jelly Shots

Serves 20

1 packet orange jelly crystals
200 ml (7 fl oz) boiling water
100 ml (3½ fl oz) fresh orange juice
100 ml (3½ fl oz) vodka
90 ml (⅓ cup) green ginger wine
2 passionfruit, pulped

Dissolve jelly crystals in boiling water. Stir in orange juice then leave to cool for five minutes. Add vodka, green ginger wine and passionfruit pulp, mixing well. Pour into shot glasses and refrigerate to set, preferably overnight.

Mango Daiquiri Jelly Shots

Serves 20

1 packet mango jelly crystals
300 ml (1½ cups) boiling water
1 mango, pureed
90 ml (⅓ cup) Bacardi
60 ml (¼ cup) Cointreau

Dissolve jelly crystals in boiling water. Pour into blender with pureed mango, blend then add alcohol and blend again. Pour into shot glasses and refrigerate to set, preferably overnight.

Blackberry and Lychee Jelly Shots

Serves 20

1 packet blackberry jelly crystals
200 ml (7 fl oz) of boiling water
½ of 200 g (7 oz) can lychees, chopped, with juice
½ punnet blackberries, chopped
100 ml (3½ fl oz) cranberry juice
90 ml (⅓ cup) vodka
45 ml (1½ fl oz) Cointreau

Dissolve jelly crystals in boiling water. Stir in finely chopped fruit and juices, then alcohol. Pour into shot glasses and refrigerate to set, preferably overnight.

Tequila Sunrise Jelly Shots

Serves 20

1 packet orange jelly crystals
250 ml (1 cup) boiling water
125 ml (½ cup) Tequila
130 ml (4½ fl oz) orange juice with pulp
30 ml (1 fl oz) Grenadine or raspberry cordial

Dissolve jelly crystals in boiling water. Stir in Tequila and orange juice, mixing well. Separate 60 g (2 oz) of the mixture and stir in Grenadine. Pour into shot glasses then refrigerate to set for half an hour, leaving remaining mixture at room temperature. After half an hour check that jelly in refrigerator has started to set, if so pour the orange layer onto the red layer creating separate layers. Put completed jelly shots into the refrigerator to set, preferably overnight.

Blackberry and
Lychee Jelly Shots

Apple, Cherry and Strawberry Jelly Shots

Apple, Cherry and Strawberry Jelly Shots

Serves 20

1 packet cherry jelly crystals
200 ml (7 fl oz) boiling water
150 ml (2/3 cup) apple juice
Juice and pulp of 1 lime
½ punnet strawberries, chopped
75 ml (2½ fl oz) vodka
75 ml (2½ fl oz) Cointreau

Dissolve jelly crystals in boiling water. Stir in juices then the strawberries and alcohol. Pour into shot glasses and refrigerate to set, preferably overnight.

Tropical Twist Jelly Shots

Serves 20

1 packet tropical jelly crystals
200 ml (7 fl oz) boiling water
100 ml (3½ fl oz) tropical fruit juice
Pulp of 1 passionfruit
90 ml (1/3 cup) Bacardi
60 ml (¼ cup) Cointreau

Dissolve jelly crystals in boiling water. Stir in juice then passionfruit and alcohol. Pour into shot glasses and refrigerate to set, preferably overnight.

Fruit Fiesta Jelly Shots

Serves 20

1 packet tropical fruit jelly crystals
200 ml (7 fl oz) boiling water
1 banana, pureed
1 lime, pulped
125 ml (½ cup) Bacardi
150 ml (⅔ cup) apple juice

Dissolve jelly crystals in boiling water. Pour into blender with pureed banana and lime pulp, blend then add alcohol and apple juice, then blend again. Pour into shot glasses and refrigerate to set, preferably overnight.

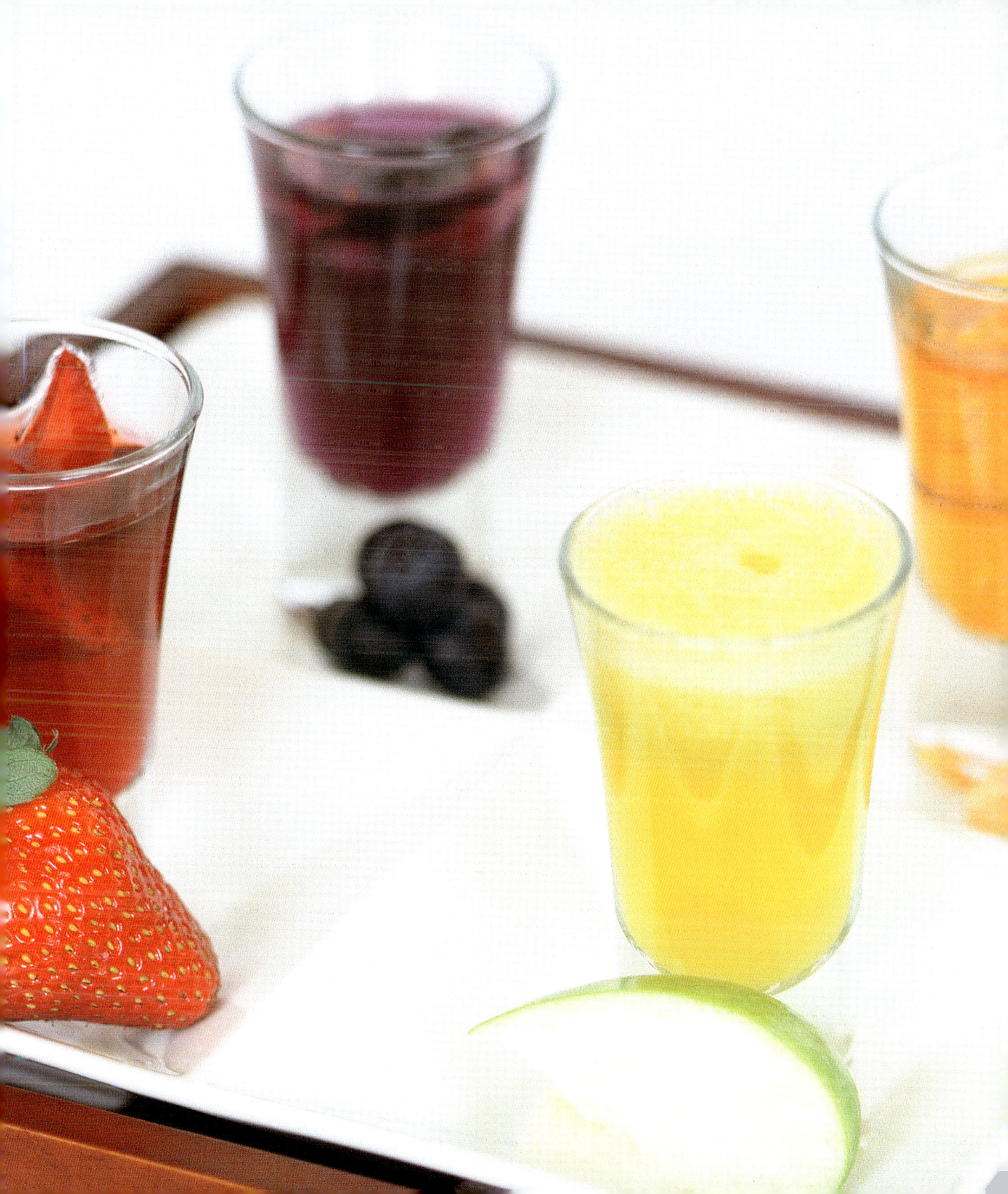

Coffee treats

The fragrant aroma of coffee blended with a subtle dash of strong liqueur. Guaranteed to get your guests smiling.

Mexican Coffee

Serves 4

2 tablespoons brown sugar
1 teaspoon vanilla essence
1 litre (4 cups) hot percolated coffee
125 ml (½ cup) Kahlua
30 ml (1 fl oz) Tequila (optional)
150 ml (2/3 cup) double cream

Add brown sugar and vanilla essence to the coffee and stir until the sugar has dissolved. Stir in the Kahlua and Tequila (if using) then divide mixture into four heat-resistant glasses. Hold a spoon just above the surface of each coffee, pour the cream very slowly down the back of the spoon so it forms a pool on the top. Serve at once.

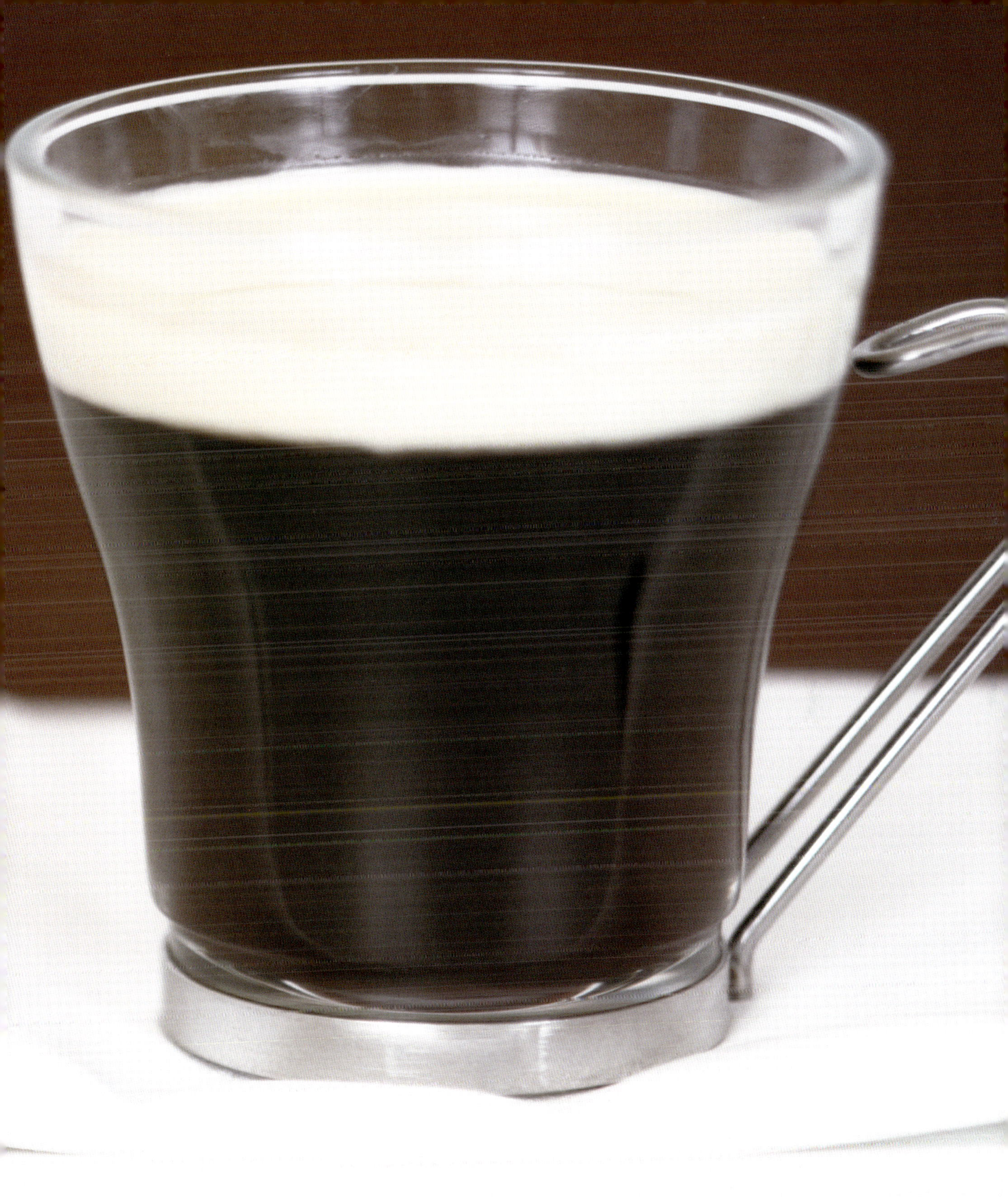

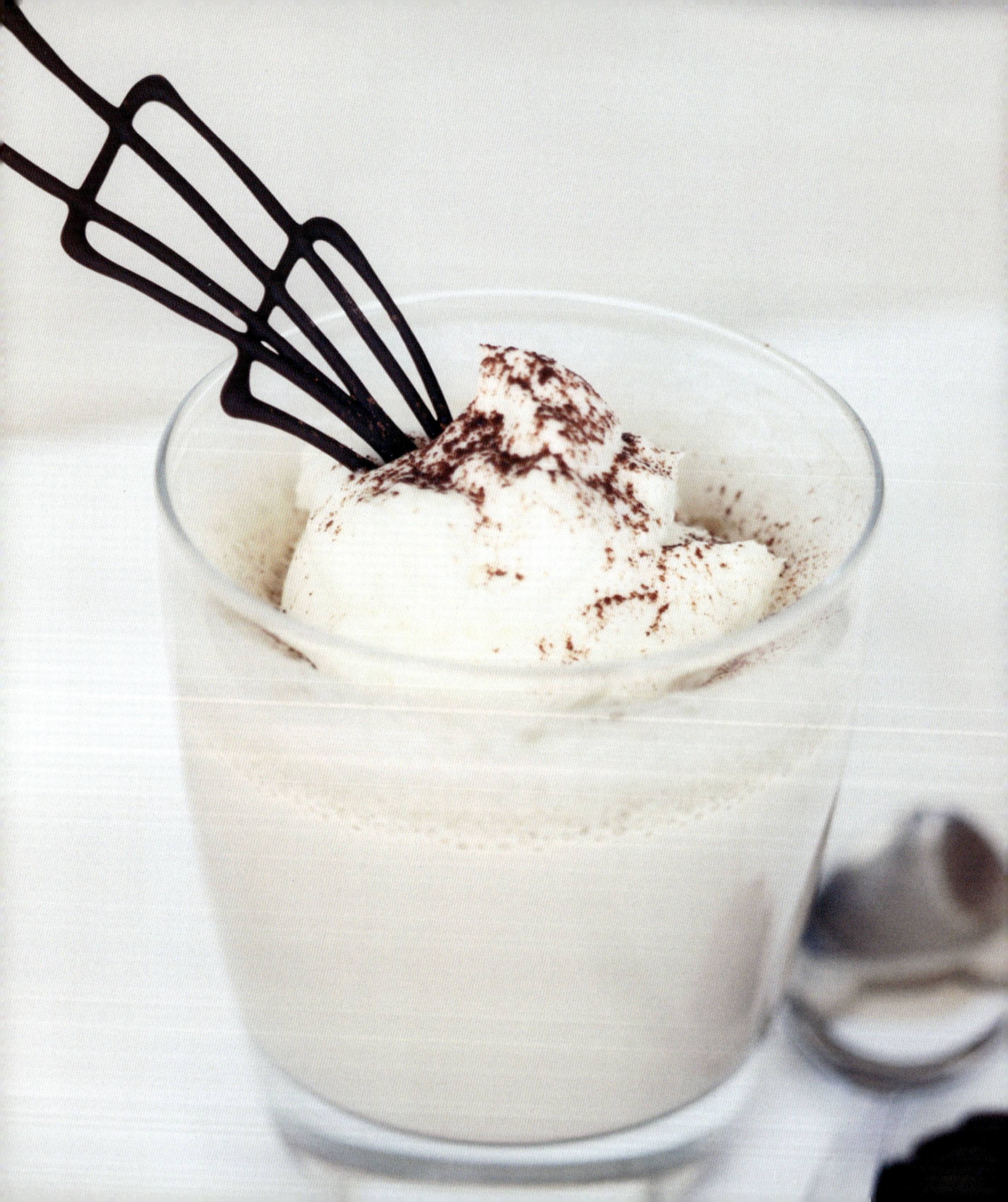

Baileys Irish Cream Coffee Mousse

Serves 6

1 sachet gelatin
250 ml (1 cup) hot coffee
150 ml (2/3 cup) cream
125 ml (½ cup) Baileys Irish Cream
1 tablespoon brown sugar
Whipped cream and chocolate shavings to garnish

Dissolve gelatin in hot coffee, allow to cool. Place cream, Baileys and sugar in a blender, lightly blend. Add cooled coffee and gelatin mix, blend well. Pour into small latte glasses and refrigerate to set. Garnish with whipped cream and chocolate shavings.

Cointreau Coffee Mousse

Serves 6

Note: These desserts set differently every time you make them. Depending on the consistency of the coffee and the cream you may find they layer or set as one; either way they taste great.

1 sachet gelatin
250 ml (1 cup) hot coffee
150 ml (2/3 cup) cream
90 ml (1/3 cup) Cointreau
1 tablespoon brown sugar
Whipped cream and chocolate shavings to garnish

Dissolve gelatin in hot coffee, allow to cool. Place cream, Cointreau and sugar in a blender, lightly blend. Add cooled coffee gelatin mix, blend well. Pour into small latte glasses and refrigerate to set. Garnish with whipped cream and chocolate shavings.

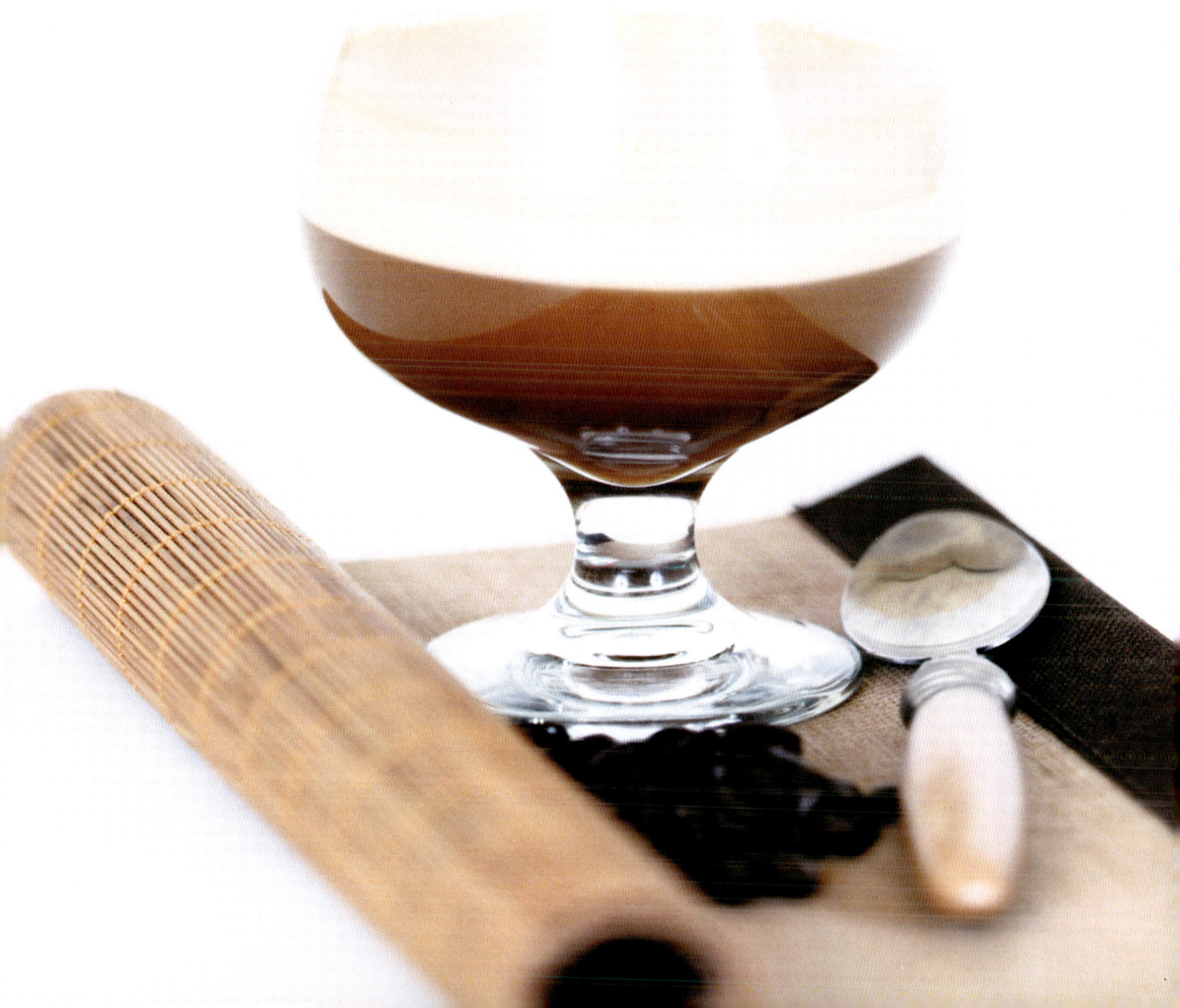

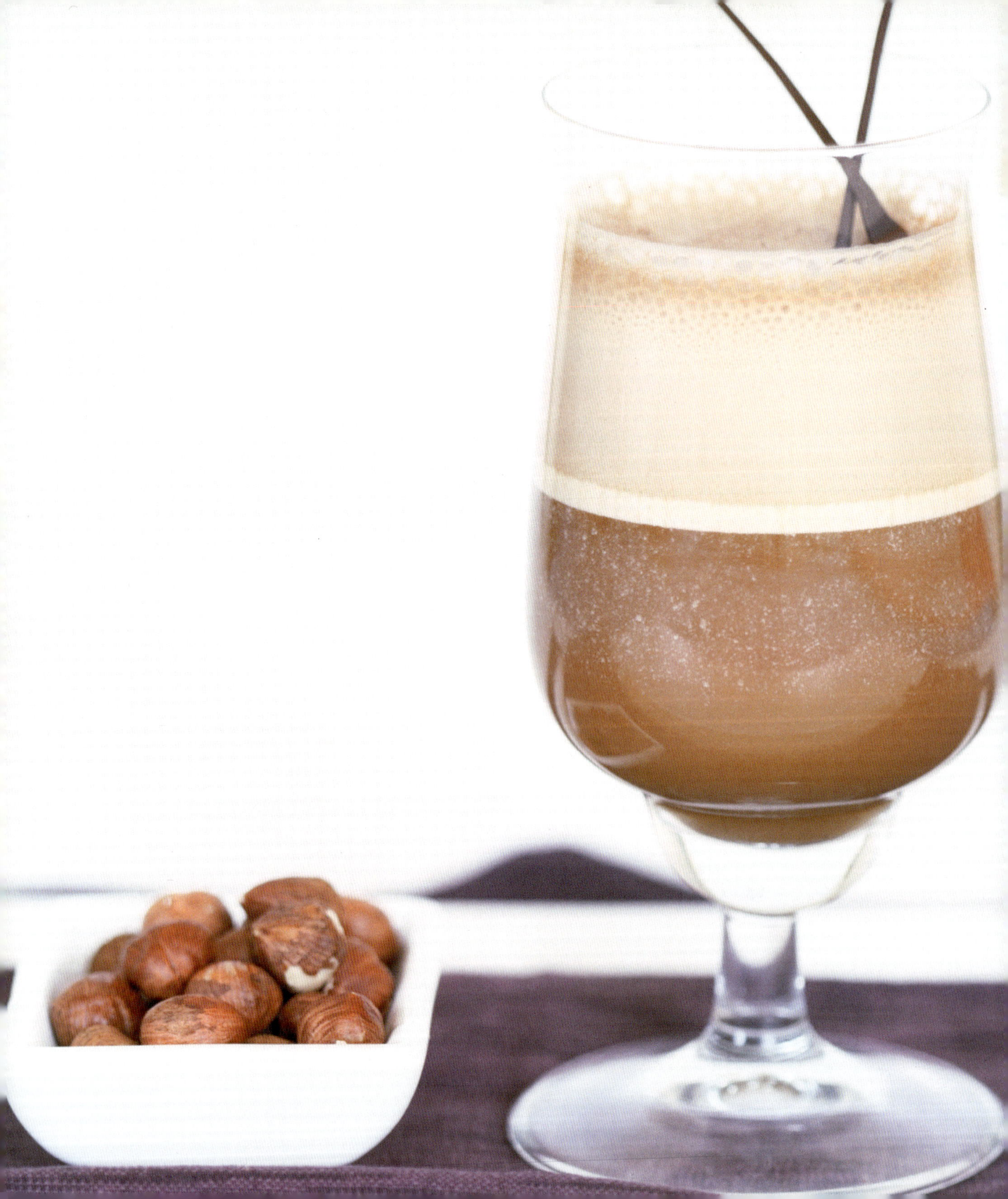

Hazelnut Coffee Mousse

Serves 6

Dissolve gelatin in hot coffee, allow to cool. Place cream, Kahlua, Frangelico and sugar in a blender, lightly blend. Add cooled coffee gelatin mix, blend well. Pour into small latte glasses and refrigerate to set. Garnish with whipped cream and chocolate shavings.

Note: These desserts set differently every time you make them. Depending on the consistency of the coffee and the cream you may find they layer or set as one; either way they taste great.

1 sachet gelatin
250 ml (1 cup) hot coffee
150 ml (2/3 cup) cream
60 ml (¼ cup) Kahlua
60 ml (¼ cup) Frangelico
1 tablespoon brown sugar
Whipped cream and chocolate shavings to garnish

Cointreau Mocha Latte

Serves 6

Layer 1
1 sachet gelatin
1 tablespoon brown sugar
400 ml (1¾ cups) coffee
75 ml (2½ fl oz) Cointreau

Layer 2
1 x 85 g (3 oz) packet instant chocolate pudding mix
400 ml (1¾ cups) milk
100 ml (3½ fl oz) Crème de Cacao
100 ml (3½ fl oz) Baileys Irish Cream

Layer 3
250 ml (1 cup) cream
Chocolate powder or shaved chocolate to garnish

Layer 1: Dissolve gelatin and sugar in hot coffee then stir in Cointreau. Pour into latte glasses, just below half full. Place in the refrigerator to set.

Layer 2: In a blender, process all ingredients until smooth. Pour onto partially set jelly so that latte glasses are now approximately 1 cm (½ in) below the top.

Layer 3: Beat cream until almost thick, not stiff. Using a plastic bag with a small section of the corner cut out, pipe the cream onto the top of the latte glasses then dust with chocolate powder or garnish with shaved chocolate.

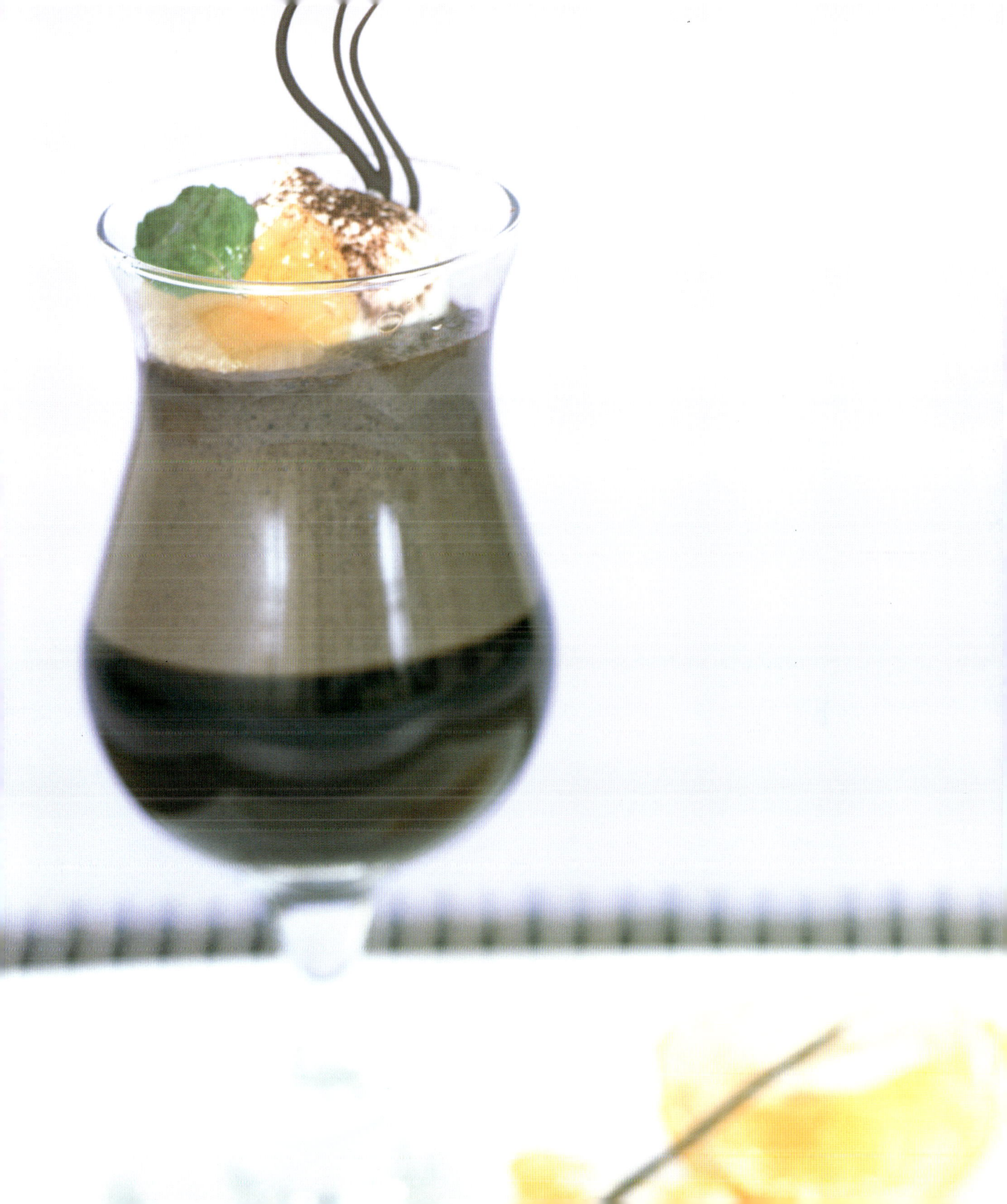

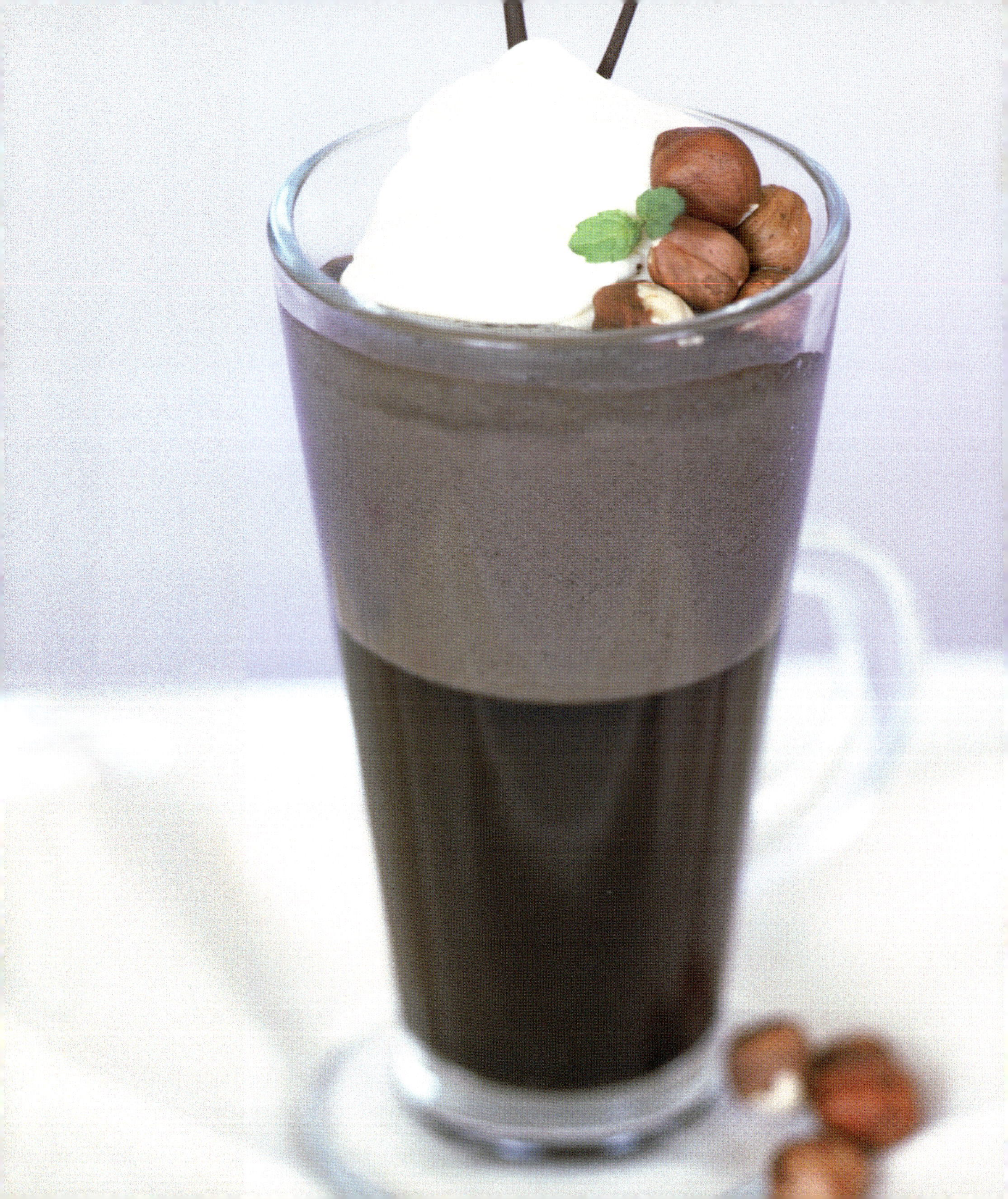

Frangelico Mocha Latte

Serves 6

Layer 1
1 sachet gelatin
1 tablespoon brown sugar
400 ml (1¾ cups) coffee
100 ml (3½ fl oz) Frangelico

Layer 2
1 x 85 g (3 oz) packet instant chocolate pudding mix
400 ml (1¾ cups) milk
100 ml (3½ fl oz) Crème de Cacao
100 ml (3½ fl oz) Baileys Irish Cream

Layer 3
250 ml (1 cup) cream
Chocolate powder or shaved chocolate to garnish

Layer 1: Dissolve gelatin and sugar in hot coffee then stir in Frangelico. Pour into latte glasses, just below half full. Place in the refrigerator to set.

Layer 2: In a blender, process all ingredients until smooth. Pour onto partially set jelly so that latte glasses are now approximately 1cm (½ in) below the top. Refrigerate to set.

Layer 3: Beat cream until almost thick, not stiff. Using a plastic bag with a small section of the corner cut out, pipe the cream onto the top of the latte glasses then dust with chocolate powder or garnish with shaved chocolate.

Peanut Butter Delight

Serves 6

Note: These desserts set differently every time you make them. Depending on the consistency of the coffee and the cream you may find they layer or set as one; either way they taste great.

1 sachet gelatin
2 tablespoons brown sugar
300 ml (1½ cups) hot percolated coffee
3 tablespoons peanut butter
90 ml (⅓ cup) Baileys Irish Cream
60 ml (¼ cup) Crème de Cacao
30 ml (1 fl oz) cream
Whipped cream and chocolate sprinkles to garnish

Dissolve gelatin and sugar in hot percolated coffee. While still hot, add peanut butter and whisk with a hand beater; the peanut butter will create a speckled effect. Add Baileys Irish Cream, Crème de Cacao and cream and whisk again. Pour mixture into individual latte glasses filled to 1 cm (½ in) below the top. Garnish with whipped cream and chocolate sprinkles.

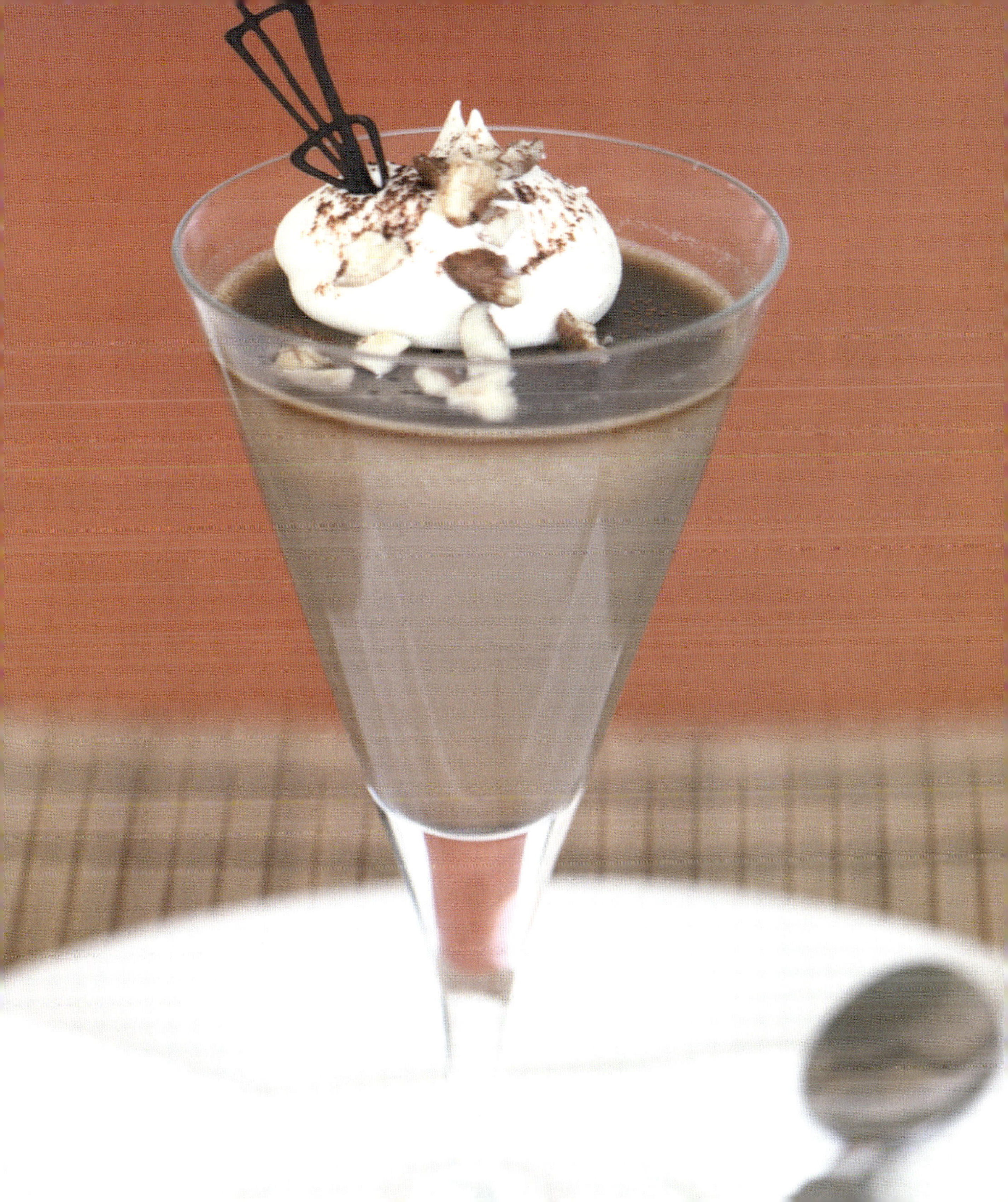

Glossary of alcoholic beverages

Bacardi	white rum
Baileys Irish Cream	a blend of cream and Irish whiskey
Blue Curacao	a clear liqueur with a mandarin-orange flavour
brandy	distilled grape wine, or spirits distilled from any fermented fruit. Some fruit liqueurs are labelled as brandies, but aren't really brandies because they are not distilled from fruit
butterscotch schnapps	butterscotch brandy
Campari	bitter, orange and herb-flavoured liqueur
Chambord	raspberry liqueur
Champagne	sparkling wine, usually white, from the Champagne district in France
Cointreau	sweet and bitter orange liqueur
Crème de Cacao	chocolate liqueur
Crème de Cassis	blackberry liqueur
Crème de Menthe	mint liqueur
Drambuie	Scotch liqueur flavoured with herbs and honey
Frangelico	hazelnut liqueur
Galliano	vanilla and anise liqueur
gin	white spirit flavoured with juniper berries, lemon and coriander seeds
Grand Marnier	orange liqueur made with cognac (brandy)
green ginger wine	wine flavoured with spirit-infused ginger
Kahlua	a blend of coffee, vanilla and rum
liqueur	fruits steeped in distilled spirits to create a sweet, alcoholic drink that is usually served after a meal, and used in desserts and sauces. Some examples of flavours available are banana, strawberry and mango

liquor	alcohol that is distilled rather than fermented
Malibu	Caribbean white rum with coconut
Midori	melon liqueur
Orange Curacao	orange liqueur
Paraiso	lychee liqueur
schnapps	a generic term for all white (clear) brandies distilled from fermented fruits. Schnapps is both fermented and distilled, whereas liqueurs are simply fruits steeped in an alcohol that has already been fermented and distilled
spirit	alcoholic beverages (such as brandy, rum, gin, whiskey, vodka) produced by distillation; usually blended with other ingredients
Tia Maria	coffee liqueur
vodka	a clear spirit, usually distilled from grain and fermented, distilled to a high proof, filtered, diluted and bottled
whiskey	aged grain alcohol fermented from malt or grain, distilled and aged in wooden barrels (which gives it its brown colour)

Index

Apple, Cherry and Strawberry Jelly Shots 137
apple schnapps 59
Apple Strudel Sorbet 59

Bacardi 39, 49, 105, 133, 137, 138
Baileys-infused Strawberries 110
Baileys Irish Cream 9, 15, 17, 23, 44, 47, 55, 110, 116, 119, 120, 145, 150, 153, 154
    Baileys Irish Cream and Coffee Ice-cream 47
    Baileys Irish Cream cheesecake 9
    Baileys Irish Cream Coffee Mousse 145
    Baileys Irish Cream Ice-cream 44
Banana Ice-cream 50
banana liqueur 50, 125
Berry Royale Jelly Shots 133
Black Forest Cheesecake 10
Blackberry and Lychee Jelly Shots 134
Blackcurrant Jelly Shots 128
Blue Curacao 105
brandy 88
Bread and Butter Pudding, Chocolate 74
Butterscotch and Chocolate Mousse Shots 116
Butterscotch Ice-cream 55
butterscotch liqueur 15, 55, 116
butterscotch schnapps 15, 55, 116

cakes, Chocolate Gateau 79
Campari 113, 132
Campari Jelly Shots 132
Chambord 20, 64, 84, 124, 133
champagne 130, 133
cheesecakes
    Baileys Irish Cream cheesecake 9
    Black Forest Cheesecake 10
    Choc Mint Cheesecake 17
    Frangelico Cheesecake 12
    Ginger, Lychee and Orange Cheesecake 24
    Honeycomb Cheesecake 15

    Mixed Berry Cheesecake 20
    Strawberries, Cointreau and Cream Cheesecake 18
    Toblerone Cheesecake 23
cherry brandy 83, 119
Cherry Ripe Mousse Shots 119
Cherry Ripe Trifle 83
Chi Chi Jelly Shots 132
Choc Mint Cheesecake 17
Choc Mint Mousse Shots 119
Chocolate and Fruit Fondue 95
Chocolate Bread and Butter Pudding 74
Chocolate Gateau 79
Chocolate Ice-cream 43
Coffee, Mexican 142
Cointreau 18, 36, 71, 73, 84, 89, 90, 91, 95, 96, 102, 106, 109, 128, 132, 133, 134, 137, 146, 150
    Cointreau and Strawberry Sorbet 36
    Cointreau Coffee Mousse 146
    Cointreau-infused Strawberries 109
    Cointreau Mocha Latte 150
Cosmopolitan Jelly Shots 128
Crème de Cacao 10, 17, 23, 33, 43, 47, 72, 74, 79, 83, 119, 150, 153, 154
Crème de Cassis 10, 80, 128
Crème de Menthe 17, 119
crepes
    Crepe Batter 88
    Crepes with Chocolate Sauce 88
    Crepes with Cointreau Cream Sauce 90
    Crepes with Toffee Sauce 88
    Lemon and Cointreau Sauce 91
Crumble, Pear and Chambord 64

Drambuie 116

Fondue, Chocolate and Fruit 95
Fondue, Fruit and Toffee Sauce 92
Frangelico 12, 23, 33, 59, 60, 67, 71, 74, 120, 149, 153
    Frangelico, Kiwi Fruit and Lime Sorbet 60
    Frangelico Cheesecake 12

Frangelico Mocha Latte   153
Freeze, Strawberry and Lychee Cream   40
Freeze, Tropical Grand Marnier   35
Fruit and Toffee Sauce Fondue   92
Fruit Fiesta Jelly Shots   138
Fruit Platter with Cointreau Cream Sauce   96

Galliano and Champagne Jelly Shots   130
gin   113, 132
Ginger, Lychee and Orange Cheesecake   24
Ginger Log   71
Grand Marnier   35, 89, 92, 95, 101
Grapefruit and Campari Sorbet   113
green ginger wine   133
Grenadine   134

Hazelnut Coffee Mousse   149
Honey, Cream and Cinnamon Ice-cream   29
Honeycomb Cheesecake   15
Honeydew Melon Delight   106

ice-cream
    Baileys Irish Cream and Coffee Ice-cream   47
    Creamy Baileys Irish Cream Ice-cream   44
    Creamy Banana Ice-cream   50
    Creamy Butterscotch Ice-cream   55
    Creamy Chocolate Ice-cream   43
    Creamy Strawberry Ice-cream   52
    Honey, Cream and Cinnamon Ice-cream   29
    Swiss Chocolate Ice-cream   33
    White Chocolate and Coconut Ice-cream   30

jelly shots
    Apple, Cherry and Strawberry Jelly Shots   137
    Berry Royale Jelly Shots   133
    Blackberry and Lychee Jelly Shots   134
    Blackcurrant Jelly Shots   128
    Campari Jelly Shots   132
    Chi Chi Jelly Shots   132
    Cosmopolitan Jelly Shots   128
    Fresh Peach Jelly Shots   130

Fruit Fiesta Jelly Shots   138
Galliano and Champagne Jelly Shots   130
Mango Daiquiri Jelly Shots   133
Midori Splice Jelly Shots   132
Orange, Ginger and Passionfruit
    Jelly Shots   133
Tequila Sunrise Jelly Shots   134
Tropical Twist Jelly Shots   137

Kahlua   71, 89, 95, 120, 142, 149

Liquid Ecstasy Pineapple Boat   105

Macadamia and Hazelnut Tart   67
Malibu   30, 39, 83, 105, 119, 132
Mango Daiquiri Jelly Shots   133
mango liqueur   124
Medos Honey Vodka   29, 125
Mexican Coffee   142
Midori   56, 105, 106, 132
Midori and Honeydew Melon Sorbet   56
Midori Splice Jelly Shots   132
Mixed Berry Cheesecake   20
Mocha Custard Delights   120
mousse
    Baileys Irish Cream Coffee Mousse   145
    Cointreau Coffee Mousse   146
    Hazelnut Coffee Mousse   149

Orange, Ginger and Passionfruit Jelly Shots 133
Orange and Lychee Daiquiri Bomb   49
Orange Curacao   24
orange liqueur   130
Orange Slices, Spiced   101

Paraiso   24, 40, 49
Parfait, Wildberry Whirl   84
Pavlova with Chocolate Cream   72
Pavlova with Cointreau Cream   73
Peach Jelly Shots   130
peach liqueur   130

Peanut Butter Delight 154
Pear and Chambord Crumble 64
Pears in Sweet White Wine 77
Pina Colada Sorbet 39
Pineapple Boat, Liquid Ecstasy 105

Scotch whisky 116
Scottish Mousse Shots 116
shots
    Butterscotch and Chocolate Mousse Shots 116
    Cherry Ripe Mousse Shots 119
    Choc-mint Mousse Shots 119
    Mocha Custard Delights 120
    Scottish Mousse Shots 116
    Vanilla, Honey and Cinnamon
        Mousse Shots 125
    Vanilla, Peach and Mango Mousse Shots 124
    Vanilla and Banana Mousse Shots 125
    Vanilla and Blackberry Mousse Shots 124
    Vanilla and Frangelico Mousse Shots 120
    Vanilla and Strawberry Mousse Shots 123
sorbets
    Apple Strudel Sorbet 59
    Cointreau and Strawberry Sorbet 36
    Frangelico, Kiwi Fruit and Lime Sorbet 60
    Grapefruit and Campari Sorbet 113
    Midori and Honeydew Melon Sorbet 56
    Pina Colada Sorbet 39
Spiced Orange Slices 101
strawberries
    Strawberries, Baileys-infused 110
    Strawberries, Cointreau and Cream Cheesecake 118
    Strawberries, Cointreau-infused 109
    Strawberry and Blackcurrant Trifle 80
    Strawberry and Lychee Cream Freeze 40
    Strawberry Ice-cream 52
    strawberry liqueur 18, 36, 40, 52, 80, 102, 123
Swiss Chocolate Ice-cream 33

Tart, Macadamia and Hazelnut 67
Tequila 134, 142

Tequila Sunrise Jelly Shots 134
Tia Maria 68, 71, 79, 89, 95
    Tia Maria Log 68
Toblerone Cheesecake 23
trifle
    Trifle, Cherry Ripe 83
    Trifle, Strawberry and Blackcurrant 80
Tropical Grand Marnier Freeze 35
Tropical Twist Jelly Shots 137

vanilla
    Vanilla, Honey and Cinnamon
        Mousse Shots 125
    Vanilla, Peach and Mango
        Mousse Shots 124
    Vanilla and Banana Mousse Shots 125
    Vanilla and Blackberry Mousse Shots 124
    Vanilla and Frangelico Mousse Shots 120
    Vanilla and Strawberry Mousse Shots 123
vodka 28, 93, 125, 128, 132, 133, 134, 137

Watermelon Boat 102
White Chocolate and Coconut Ice-cream 30
Wildberry Whirl Parfait 84
Wine, Poached Pears in 77